THE TURKEY IS NOT THE
ONLY THING GETTING
ROASTED

THE TURKEY IS NOT THE ONLY THING GETTING ROASTED

ROBERT OKINE

The Turkey Is Not The Only Thing Getting Roasted
A State-by-State Roast of Thanksgiving Chaos Across America
© 2025 Robert Okine

Published by **Fifty Options Press™**

The Turkey Is Not The Only Thing Getting Roasted is part of the **USA The Land With At Least 50 Options™** series — a humorous nonfiction collection exploring American life, culture, and collective dysfunction, one themed experience at a time.

This is a work of satire, humor, and cultural commentary.

While it draws inspiration from real regions, family archetypes, and side dish choices, all content is original, exaggerated, and lovingly fictionalized for entertainment purposes. Any resemblance to your relatives, your casserole, or your 2012 Thanksgiving meltdown is purely coincidental... and possibly overdue for resolution.

Cover design, layout, and formatting by **Robert Okine** and creative collaborators using AI-assisted tools, emotional stuffing, and three kinds of butter.

Published in the United States of America.

First Edition, 2025

For speaking, collaborations, or unsolicited apologies for anything that happened after grace: **www.therobertokine.com**

To every family that's ever argued over pie, burned a turkey, passed a dish with side-eye, or silently judged the stuffing.

You are the reason this book exists.
You are also the reason we need a nap after dinner.

Acknowledgments

This book wouldn't exist without:

- Every chaotic Thanksgiving table I've ever sat at (or heard about)

- The family members who show up with drama and dessert — in equal portions

- Friends who encouraged me to turn these stories into something roast-worthy

- Anyone who has ever said, "*You should write a book.*" (You were right. Also, now you owe me a slice of pie.)

To the readers: thank you for seeing your people in these pages — the loud ones, the weird ones, the ones who eat dessert first. May this book sit on your coffee table, gift list, and heart for years to come.

And finally...
To every turkey that didn't survive the test kitchen, you were deeply... deeply overcooked.

Pull Up a Chair

Let's be honest — Thanksgiving is not just about gratitude.
It's about **gravy, grudges, group texts gone wrong**, and someone yelling *"We're eating at 3"* when you know full well it's 6:17 p.m.

It's the most chaotic, carb-loaded, emotionally layered holiday in America.
And yet... we love it.

We show up every year — with new opinions, old recipes, unresolved issues, and just enough whipped cream to keep it civil. And for one glorious, gravy-drenched moment, we pretend we're normal.

This book is for that moment.

And every absurd one before and after it.

You're holding a **state-by-state roast** of Thanksgiving culture across the U.S. — with all its awkward toasts, mystery casseroles, and passive-aggressive pies.
One chapter per state.
One chaotic family gathering at a time.

If you see your uncle in here, don't tell him.
If you see *yourself* in here... welcome. You belong at this table.

Now take a seat.
Dinner is served.

Contents

Where the Turkey Isn't the Only Thing Roasted

You can learn a lot about a country by how it eats together.
And in America, no meal says more than Thanksgiving.

Other holidays come with rules. Or decorations. Or religious rituals.

Thanksgiving?
It comes with **expectations** — emotional, generational, culinary, and completely unrealistic.

You're supposed to gather people from multiple generations, belief systems, dietary preferences, and decades of unresolved tension into one house — and expect everything to go smoothly?

Please.

But we try anyway.
Because under the drama, the distractions, and the dry stuffing, there's something deeply human about Thanksgiving.
Something funny. Something broken. Something real.

This book isn't a collection of polished traditions.
It's a *state-by-state rollercoaster* of what really happens when Amer-

ica gives thanks — loud uncles, late casseroles, uninvited exes, Wi-Fi outages, and emotional landmines hidden in every side dish.

Fifty states.
One bonus chaos capital (we see you, D.C.).
And one truth at the center of it all:

No matter where you go in America, Thanksgiving is deliciously dysfunctional — and completely unforgettable.

So grab a fork.
Loosen your waistband.
And get ready to laugh your way across a country where the turkey isn't the only thing getting roasted.

1

Alabama — Blessings, Biscuits, and a Broken Window

Thanksgiving in Alabama always started the same way: **Biscuits, butter, and Bible verses.**
And every year, Grandma Pearl asked her three adult sons to "behave, or eat in the truck."

This year, the table was set, the turkey was perfect, and Aunt Charlene brought her *"famous"* sweet tea in a mason jar with her name on it — literally Sharpie'd on the glass.

"Y'all know I got trust issues," she said.

Everything was going fine until Cousin Troy pulled out his phone during grace... to check football scores.

Grandma didn't say a word.
She just reached over, plucked the phone from his hand, and **gently frisbee'd it out the dining room window.**

"Jesus gets five minutes, Troy."

Silence.

Then Uncle Billy laughed.
Then Aunt Charlene spit sweet tea across the candied yams.
Then Grandpa, who hadn't spoken since 2006, muttered:

"That's why I married her."

After grace, things settled... until the *Great Biscuit Debate* began.

Aunt Doris had brought *canned* biscuits.
Which, in this family, is a **culinary felony.**

"They're buttery!" she insisted.
"They're betrayal with a crust," Grandma replied.

Ten minutes later, Doris stormed out with her tray.
The dog followed her.
The dog chose canned biscuits.

But the real explosion came during the "What are you thankful for?" round.

Everyone went around the table saying nice things like:

- "Health."

- "Family."

- "Having survived 2024."

Then Cousin LaToya stood up.

"I'm thankful," she said, "that Aunt Charlene's not driving this year. Because last year she took us on a detour through her divorce, her speeding ticket, and three therapy appointments she says she doesn't need."

Charlene blinked.
Set down her cornbread.
And whispered:

"Pass me the yams before I pass judgment."

The meal ended peacefully... ish.
A window was broken.
Two casseroles went untouched.
And Grandma Pearl said she'd "pray for everyone — but not today."

In Alabama, Thanksgiving isn't just about family.
It's about hierarchy, history, and hushpuppies.
And if you don't behave, you eat in the truck.

2

Alaska — Cold Turkey and Cryogenic Cranberry Sauce

In Alaska, Thanksgiving isn't just a holiday. It's a logistical mission.

This year, the Whitaker family in Fairbanks had prepped for *everything*:

- A backup generator

- A snowmobile delivery from Costco

- Three turkeys (just in case)

What they didn't prep for?
Todd.
Cousin Todd.

Back from six months in the wilderness with a beard, a GoPro, and a strict new diet:

"Only what I can catch or ferment."

He brought pickled salmon... in a jar he sealed with duct tape.

Dinner started at 3:00 p.m. sharp.
By 3:07, the cranberry sauce had frozen on the plate like a Jell-O sculpture mid-panic attack.
The mashed potatoes had to be microwaved three times.
And the gravy?
Poured like concrete.

Todd pulled out a knife (his own — not from the kitchen) to "carve the spirit of the bird."
No one asked what that meant.
They just passed the rolls.

But the real drama came when Aunt Carrie announced she was *moving to Arizona.*

"I'm tired of eating in parkas," she said.
"And I'd like my wine to stay liquid at room temperature."

Uncle Dave took this personally.
He stood up mid-bite and said:

"If you can't handle a little chill, maybe you've been in the *Lower 48* too long."

Someone gasped.

Someone else opened a beer.

Grandma slid the frozen cranberry sculpture slowly off the table.

Dessert was a store-bought pumpkin pie that had thawed un-evenly.

The middle was cold.

The edges were burnt.

Todd called it "a metaphor for modern civilization."

No one knew what that meant either.

In Alaska, the turkey isn't the only thing that needs defrosting. But somehow, even when the sides are cold and the family's colder... they show up anyway.

3

Arizona — Cactus Salad and Commitment Issues

Thanksgiving in Scottsdale was already off to a spicy start, and not just because someone replaced the stuffing with jalapeño cornbread again.

This year, **Janelle** brought a new fiancé.
Her *third* in five years.
His name? **Chase.**
Occupation? **Crypto startup evangelist.**
Footwear? **Leather flip-flops.**

"We met at a cacao ceremony in Sedona," Janelle said.
"He's in alignment with my root chakra."

No one knew what that meant.
But Grandma whispered, *"We miss fiancé number two. He brought sangria."*

As dinner started, Chase offered to "bless the meal with intentional vibrations."
He pulled out a tuning fork.
A **tuning fork**.

While he rang it over the cranberry sauce, Uncle Rob muttered:

"Well, now it's blessed and awkward."

Then came the **cactus salad.**

Janelle brought it in a reclaimed wood bowl, announced it was "inspired by ancestral desert traditions," and passed it with a smirk.

One bite in, Grandpa started sweating.
By bite two, he asked for milk.
There was no milk.
There was only **almond creamer** and **a turmeric smoothie** Chase had brought "for post-meal detox."

The kids were eating mac and cheese.
From a box.
No shame. Just survival.

Meanwhile, Aunt Becky tried to steer the conversation toward "things we're grateful for," but Chase interrupted:

"I'm grateful that I've finally found a space where my masculine energy isn't repressed."

No one responded.
But someone coughed *"testosterone tofu"* into their napkin.

When dessert arrived (store-bought pie, because "the oven was on a spiritual break"), Chase announced he and Janelle were eloping... in a yurt.

Grandpa whispered, "Make it number four."
No one laughed.
But everyone nodded.

In Arizona, Thanksgiving heat doesn't just come from the chili flakes.
Sometimes it comes from sage-burning, salad drama, and the sound of a tuning fork echoing across your patience.

4

Arkansas — Squirrel Stew and Selective Memory

Thanksgiving in Little Rock started with the usual:
hugs, hats, and someone yelling, *"Who parked in the yard?!"*

Grandma Dottie was already in the kitchen doing what she
does best:
Yelling lovingly.

"If you're not bringing food, bring silence!"

Everything was running smooth(ish)...
Until Uncle Dwight rolled in with **a giant Crock-Pot** and a proud
grin.

"Got a little surprise this year," he said, lifting the lid.
"Family recipe."

Inside: brown liquid, mystery chunks, and three floating bay leaves struggling to make eye contact with anyone.

"Smells... interesting," someone muttered.

Uncle Dwight beamed.

"Squirrel stew."

SQUIRREL. STEW.

Everyone froze.

Cousin Dusty dropped his cornbread.

Aunt Lisa gripped the edge of the table so hard her knuckles went white, her potato salad momentarily forgotten.

"Whose family recipe?" Lisa asked, carefully.

"Ours," Dwight said proudly.

"From the Ozarks. Pawpaw used to trap 'em right behind the barn."

"Pawpaw also ate chalk," Dusty whispered. "And believed Elvis lived under the porch."

Grandma Dottie made an emergency pot of chili.

The Crock-Pot was pushed to the far end of the counter, next to the recycling bin and *whatever Brittani brought last year that smelled like regret.*

But that wasn't the only surprise.

Midway through dinner, cousin Lindsay — recently back from "finding herself" on a goat farm in Vermont — announced she's now **fruitarian.**

"I only eat what falls naturally from a tree," she said, holding a lone pear.

Uncle Dwight, still salty about the squirrel, muttered:

"Ain't nobody falling for that."

The pear was not eaten.
Neither was the stew.

Dessert was warm pecan pie and a very tense moment when Grandma asked if anyone had "updates on their lives that don't involve TikTok or squirrels."

No one spoke.
But someone turned up the volume on the football game.
And someone else quietly fed the stew to the neighbor's dog.

The dog lived.
But he now sleeps with one eye open and avoids anything in a Pyrex dish.

In Arkansas, Thanksgiving comes with secrets, sauce, and stew you shouldn't ask too many questions about.
If it moves, they'll Crock-Pot it.
If it's awkward, they'll bless it.
And if it's family... they'll invite it anyway.

5

California — Conscious Eating and Cranberry Drama

Thanksgiving in Los Angeles was hosted by Sierra and Jax.
They're newly engaged.
They live in a "tiny eco-loft" with no dining table, but four ring lights and a composting toilet.

This year's theme?
"Conscious Gratitude."

"Dinner's plant-based, low-carbon, and emotionally safe," Sierra announced via Instagram Live.
"Please don't bring anything with gluten, meat, or unresolved trauma."

Uncle Ramon brought ribs.
From a smoker in his truck.

He said nothing, just set them down next to the *tofurky* and dared anyone to judge him.

First red flag?
There was a **welcome meditation** before grace.
Everyone had to sit cross-legged and set an "intention."

Grandma tried, bless her.

"My intention," she whispered, eyes closed, "is for someone to bring me a damn potato."

The food was... creative.

- Vegan mac and cheese that tasted like sadness.

- Mashed cauliflower with a foam on top.

- A gluten-free pie crust made from pressed cashews and what might've been regret.

Sierra's friend Blaze (yes, Blaze) brought *activated charcoal water* and asked if the turkey was "ethically transitioned."
Uncle Ramon muttered, "*I transitioned it straight into the smoker, thanks.*"

Midway through the meal, Cousin Dani went on a tear about "how capitalism ruined cranberry sauce."

"Why are we *buying* something that grows naturally in bogs?"

She then passed around homemade raw cranberry slush in mason jars.

Someone described it as "aggressively tart."
Someone else said, "My mouth is vibrating."
No one finished it.

Things hit a new low when Blaze picked up a tuning fork and tried to "cleanse the energy around the stuffing."

The dog barked.
Someone's wine glass cracked.
Grandma went outside to sit in the Prius with the heat on.

At dessert, Sierra asked everyone to "go around and share what their inner child is thankful for."

Uncle Ramon said, "My inner child wants ribs and regular pie."
Blaze started to cry.
The livestream lost connection.

And the ribs?
Gone.

In California, Thanksgiving is organic, non-GMO, emotionally expressive... and slightly exhausting.
But at least the napkins were compostable.
And no one had to pretend the cranberry slush was good.

6

Colorado — High Altitude, Higher Expectations

Friendsgiving in Colorado was hosted by Kayla and Trent — recent transplants from Brooklyn who now live in a "converted ski-lodge-turned-conscious-community-space" near Breckenridge.

The guest list included:

- A barista-turned-life-coach

- A couple who only eats raw food

- Three rescue dogs

- One actual goat (long story)

Dinner started at 5:00 PM.
By 4:15, everyone was already a little *elevated* — and not just from the altitude.

Kayla opened with a land acknowledgment, a guided breath-work session, and a group chant.

Trent, wearing a poncho made from "reclaimed hemp," whispered:

"Let's not just eat — let's *commune*."

Then they unveiled the meal:

- Wild rice-stuffed squash

- Vegan mushroom gravy

- A "psychedelic gratitude salad" (made with microgreens and questionable microdoses)

Uncle Barry, who flew in from Denver and hadn't eaten since breakfast, leaned toward the table and said:

"So... where's the *actual* food?"

Kayla handed him a raw walnut loaf.
He stared at it like it owed him money.

As dinner went on, the room got... intense.

Someone cried over the stuffing (it reminded them of their ex's energy).
Someone else tried to get a group photo but fell off a yoga block.
The goat escaped, ate half a charcuterie board, and licked the salt lamp.

Trent said that was "symbolic."

But the peak of the evening came during the **"Circle of Raw Truths."**

Everyone had to share something vulnerable.
It was going okay — until Barry blurted out:

"I don't get any of this. I just wanted turkey and sports. Y'all out here crying into sweet potatoes."

Silence.
Then Kayla whispered:

"Thank you for your honesty."

Then River (who drove up from California because of course he did) said:

"That's brave of you, Barry. Would you like to co-facilitate my next breathwork series?"

Barry declined.
Twice.

Dessert was an avocado mousse described as "a revelation in restraint."
Barry drove to Taco Bell.

The goat slept on a beanbag chair.
Peace was declared.

In Colorado, Friendsgiving isn't just a meal — it's a journey.
Sometimes uphill. Sometimes sideways.
But always seasoned with sage, sound bowls, and someone forgetting to bring forks.

7

Connecticut — Chardonnay and Chilly Conversations

Thanksgiving in Greenwich was hosted by *Margot and Stephen*. She's a lawyer. He's in finance.
Their dining room has a chandelier, a "conversation shelf," and a **seating chart** color-coded by dietary preference *and* political affiliation.

"We want dinner to feel safe and synergistic," Margot said, passing around a printed agenda titled:
"Thanksgiving: An Elegant Harvest of Gratitude."

The appetizers were artisanal.
The conversation was... strategic.

People discussed:

- Hedge fund forecasts

- Dry-aged turkey trends

- Whether or not dry brining is "still in"

No one raised their voice.
No one talked over anyone.
And yet... **everyone was quietly furious.**

The seating chart became the first battleground.
Stephen's cousin, *Doug*, was placed at the "gluten-free buffer table."
He took it as a personal attack.

"I had ONE bagel in 2019," Doug muttered, sipping pinot noir.
"Now I'm exiled with the pescatarians?"

Meanwhile, Great Aunt Beatrice was seated between two
teenagers with matching iPads and noise-canceling headphones.

She made polite conversation anyway.
To herself.

Dinner was a five-course plated experience served in silence...
until **Uncle Richard** brought up "the estate situation."

Suddenly, forks froze midair.

"Now's not the time," Margot said, voice tight.
"I emailed a document about this in September."

Doug snorted.
Beatrice gasped.
The iPads kept streaming *Minecraft ASMR*.

Dessert came with an optional "Gratitude Reflection Card" activity.
Each person pulled a card and answered the prompt.
Some examples included:

- "What did 2024 teach you about grace?"

- "If your soul were a pie, what flavor would it be?"

Doug's card asked:

"What are you letting go of?"

He said:

"This family."

Left without touching the pear galette.

In Connecticut, Thanksgiving is quiet, curated, and probably trademarked.
But behind the monogrammed napkins and emotional detachment...
is a family trying *very, very hard* to not lose it until they get back to the car.

8

Delaware — Double-Booked and Deeply Unprepared

Thanksgiving in Dover was supposed to be chill. **Just Aunt Mel. A few cousins. One turkey.**

But thanks to a combination of:

- An old group text,

- A glitchy Evite,

- And **Mel's inability to say no,**
  two completely separate sides of the family showed up. At once.

"I thought this was *our* year to host," said her sister.
"No, *we* host on odd-numbered years," said her husband's cousin.

"It's 2025," said Mel.
"Exactly," they both replied.

Mel's face said:

"I will pretend this is fine until I am legally allowed to scream into a pillow."

The kitchen? Chaos.
There were *three* green bean casseroles.
None of them matched.
Someone brought a ham. Someone else brought a vegan lasagna.
The oven was *already* in crisis.

The turkey was dry.
The wine was flowing.
And there was a visible turf war forming between the living room and the "casual seating zone."

Tension peaked during "grace."

Each side assumed **they** were leading it.
Both grandmothers stood up at the same time.
Neither sat down.

"Lord, we thank you—"
"We bless this house—"
"This isn't YOUR house, it's Mel's—"
"Well she uses MY stuffing recipe, so—"

Mel coughed aggressively, pointed to the cranberry sauce, and said,

"Let's just... eat, before it gelatinizes more."

During dinner, Uncle Glenn tried to lead a *"fun icebreaker game"* and accidentally uncovered a **shared ex** between the families.

Her name was Leslie.
She was on her second plate of mac and cheese.
And she *did not* look up.

"I think I'm gonna need more gravy," she said softly, staring into the middle distance.

By dessert, the kids had formed a unified front under the dining table with iPads and leftover rolls.

Mel was in the garage breathing into a paper bag.
Her dog was wearing a napkin like a cape and dragging the vegan lasagna tray into the laundry room.

And someone finally said what Mel had been thinking since noon:

"We should've just done a group Zoom."

In Delaware, the state may be small — but the drama multiplies fast.
Especially when *both sides of the family* bring their own mashed potatoes *and* their own definitions of forgiveness.

9

Florida — Gators, Grits,
and a Margarita Meltdown

Thanksgiving in Fort Myers was already off-script before the turkey even hit the smoker.

Why?

Because **Granddad Rick** had decided to make it a **"Margarita Thanksgiving."**

"It's too damn hot for cider," he declared at 10:45 a.m., sipping from a salt-rimmed Solo cup.

The turkey?
Still frozen.
The margaritas?
Flowing.

Guests arrived in tank tops and sandals.
Someone brought fried gator tail "as a conversation piece."

Someone else brought *pineapple on stuffing* and immediately got side-eyed into silence.

Cousin Michelle tried to organize a polite game of charades.
Uncle Kenny responded by yelling *"Florida Man!"* and doing a cannonball into the above-ground pool.
He wasn't invited.
He showed up anyway.
So did his pet iguana.

As the sun set and the margaritas multiplied, dinner was officially **two hours late**.
So people started picking at sides:

- Deviled eggs with jalapeños

- Shrimp cocktail from a bait shop

- And a suspicious casserole labeled simply: *"Brenda's Business."*

No one asked.
No one touched it.

Then came the **Great Generator Incident**.

The outdoor fryer was overloaded.
The power cut out.
The football game disappeared mid-field goal and someone screamed like they'd been shot.

Granddad Rick grabbed a flashlight and slurred:

"This is why I hate daylight savings. It steals the joy."

Brenda dropped her business casserole.
No one noticed.

Eventually, the turkey was "done."
It was dry.
It was late.
And it had absorbed just enough Florida humidity to develop... a *texture*.

Everyone ate it anyway.
With hot sauce.
And tequila.

Dessert was key lime pie served in paper bowls that began to collapse under pressure.
Cousin Michelle quietly cried during grace.
The iguana fell asleep under the table.
Uncle Kenny offered someone a tattoo he "could do right now" if they had a steady hand and no regrets.

Two people said yes.

In Florida, Thanksgiving isn't just a meal — it's a cautionary tale.
One part heat, one part rum, and a whole lot of *"Well, that escalated quickly."*

10

Georgia — Grace, Grits, and Gospel Shade

Thanksgiving in Atlanta started, as always, with **a full-on church choir warm-up.**

Why?

Because Grandma Eunice insists grace be "delivered with spirit and at least *four-part harmony.*"

So at 2:47 p.m., the meal was on pause while three aunts and a tenor cousin sang a medley of *"Total Praise"* and *"Pass Me Not, O Gentle Savior."*

There were **runs. Modulations. A tambourine.**

The turkey was cooling rapidly.

The greens were sweating.

Uncle Curtis whispered,

"Didn't we already eat at church last Sunday?"

Once seated, things looked promising:

- Mac and cheese so thick it needed a fork license

- Fried turkey with *"a little extra crunch"* (aka the fire alarm went off once)

- Cornbread dressing that made someone cry "in tongues"

Then... **Tasha walked in.**

With Jerome.
And his mama.
Unannounced.

"We were in the neighborhood," Tasha said, smiling too wide.
"Girl, this ain't a drive-thru," someone muttered.

Jerome's mama (Miss Loretta) brought her *own* sweet tea.
When Aunt Marla asked why, she said:

"I just like to be sure I'm drinking something made with *love*, not ego."

OHHH.
Even the *deviled eggs froze in fear.*

Grandma Eunice clutched her pearls.
Tasha clutched Jerome.
The tenors clutched the tambourine in case things got musical.

Dinner was a mix of *blessings and barely concealed beef.*

Loretta asked who made the grits.
No one answered.
She said,

"Thought so."
And *tossed the spoon like it was infected.*

Aunt Marla later "accidentally" spilled tea on Loretta's linen skirt.
It was described as "baptismal" and "deserved."

After dessert (pound cake so dense it bent a fork), Cousin Dev stood up for the "Thankfulness Round."
Everyone said nice things.

Then Jerome said:

"I'm thankful Tasha upgraded from y'all's family to mine."

Silence.
Then *Grandma Eunice* stood up.

"Let us pray."

The prayer was seven minutes.
Four of them were about forgiveness.
Three were *not.*

In Georgia, Thanksgiving comes with harmony, heat, and high-stakes hospitality.
You will sing.
You will smile.
And if you bring your own sweet tea... you'd better *be ready to drink the consequences.*

11

Hawaii — Leis, Lava Pits, and Lomi Lomi Tension

Thanksgiving in Maui started before sunrise.
Because Uncle Kalani insisted on **traditional imu-style turkey** — buried underground with banana leaves, hot rocks, and *four hours of ancestral expectations.*

"It's about honoring the old ways," he said.
"Also, my smoker broke."

Meanwhile, Auntie Moana was prepping her famous haupia pie and "slightly aggressive" poke platter.
And the cousins?
The cousins were *practicing a choreographed hula roast battle.*

Yes. A **hula roast battle.**
Think sass, grass skirts, and *pointed eyebrow isolation.*

Guests arrived wearing leis, flip-flops, and quiet beef.

Tensions flared when Cousin Nani showed up with her *haole* boyfriend **Chad** from Wisconsin.

"He's never had taro before," she said proudly.
"He thought it was toothpaste," someone whispered.

Chad brought boxed wine.
He poured it into a coconut and said,

"Mahalo, y'all."

The imu turkey finally emerged around 3:00 PM — perfectly steamed and *accidentally* dragged through the dirt when Uncle Kalani tripped over a sandal.

"Add some crunch," he said, brushing it off with a palm frond.

Dinner included:

- Lomi lomi salmon

- Spam musubi

- Something green labeled *"Tita's Cleanse"*

- And mac salad so good it made someone propose (again)

During grace, Grandpa Moke gave a long, meandering blessing about tides, patience, and "what we learned from that time the family canoe got repossessed."

Chad tried to clap at the end.
Nobody clapped.
Chad stopped clapping.

Dessert was three kinds of pie and one unexpected ukulele solo from Cousin Liko, who dedicated a song to "my inner child and my ex."

It was... emotional.
No one made eye contact for five whole minutes.

As the sun set, people took their leftovers, their unspoken frustrations, and one soaked hula skirt (long story) down to the beach.
The kids lit sparklers.
Chad stepped on sea urchin.
Grandma waved a ti leaf and said,

"That's what you get for putting ice in your poi."

In Hawaii, Thanksgiving is a feast, a feeling, and occasionally a full-body cultural reset.
Come with aloha. Leave with stories.
And never — *never* — bring boxed wine in a coconut.

12

Idaho — Tater Tension and the Great Roll Scandal

Thanksgiving in Boise was supposed to be peaceful.

The leaves were crisp, the turkey was golden, and Aunt Connie had made her **legendary potato casserole** — three cheeses, hand-whipped, and covered with a crust that made people weep *in gratitude.*

Then *Shelby* walked in.

Shelby, age 27. Fresh from a year in Portland.

With bangs. And *opinions.*

She set a grocery bag on the counter and pulled out a plastic container.

"I brought gluten-free kale rolls! Thought I'd lighten things up."

Silence.

Uncle Dale muttered,

"Lighten up? We're in Idaho, not on a juice cleanse."

Grandma stared at the rolls like they had personally insulted her tractor.

The meal began with polite conversation and buried rage.

The table was heavy with:

- Turkey

- Ham

- Mashed potatoes

- Baked potatoes

- Scalloped potatoes

- Potato salad

- One bowl of *green beans nobody asked for*

Shelby passed the kale rolls.
They were *touched...* but never *taken.*

Then came the moment Idaho families both fear and expect:
The **Passive-Aggressive Casserole Showdown.**

Uncle Roy took a second helping of Aunt Connie's dish.
Loudly said,

"Now *this* is what Thanksgiving's about."

Aunt Jolinda, who'd brought *her own* potato casserole with coconut milk and "a splash of innovation," smiled and said:

"That's okay. Not everyone has the palate for complexity."

Connie nodded slowly.

"Bless your heart. Maybe next year try seasoning."

Even the gravy thickened with tension.

Grace was short, sweet, and slightly shady.

Grandpa Stan said,

"Lord, thank you for family, for tradition, and for real butter."

Shelby raised her hand and said,

"Actually—"

Someone dropped a fork.
No one let her finish.

Dessert was huckleberry pie, pumpkin bars, and one leftover kale roll quietly removed from the table by a family dog named Buster.

He sniffed it.

Licked it.

Walked away.

In Idaho, Thanksgiving runs on tradition, tension, and *tubers*. Show up with something green, and you might just leave with a story.

Or a new understanding of what "Don't mess with the potatoes" really means.

13

Illinois — Tupperware
Moves and That One
Plus-One

T hanksgiving in Naperville started with a knock, a hug, and
Aunt Cheryl asking:

"Where's the foil? I brought my containers."

It was 10:47 a.m.

The turkey was still in the oven.
The prayer circle hadn't started.
And yet, Aunt Cheryl's Tupperware tower was already stacked on
the counter like she was staging a hostage exchange.

"I'm not tryna leave here hungry like last year," she whispered,
labeling a container *"Mac & Me Only."*

Then in walked **Devin** — Cousin Melissa's new boyfriend.
No warning. No intro text.
Just vibes and a Bluetooth speaker playing trap Christmas music.

"We met at Target," Melissa said.
"He's a free spirit."

Devin brought *cinnamon-infused kombucha.*
Called it "a palate cleanser."
Grandpa called it *"offensive."*

Dinner kicked off with a traditional prayer, led by Uncle Calvin, who used exactly **seven "Father Gods"** in a row and ended with:

"And please help Aunt Cheryl keep her hands off the pie before it cools this year."

She didn't blink.
She just pulled the foil off the peach cobbler like it owed her money.

At the table:

- Devin asked if the turkey was *"grass-fed emotionally."*

- Aunt Marlene replied, "It was fed to a smoker in my backyard for 9 hours. Eat it or don't."

• Aunt Cheryl scooped half the baked mac and cheese into her *"Mac & Me Only"* bin... mid-meal.

By the time dessert rolled around, tensions were **al dente.**

Then Cheryl struck again.
She took the *entire banana pudding* — bowl and all — and said:

"I'll return it at Christmas."

Aunt Latrice snatched it back so fast, her nails scraped the plastic lid.

"We will NOT do this this year."

Someone yelled,

"Worldstar!"
No one recorded.
Everyone watched.

Devin tried to lighten the mood by doing a magic trick with a dinner roll and a tea light.

He singed his eyebrow.
Melissa clapped.
Grandma said,

"Don't bring him back."

In Illinois, Thanksgiving is layered like a lasagna — hot, heavy, and full of unspoken grudges.

Come for the food, stay for the Tupperware heist, and pray no one brings a magician to dinner.

14

Indiana — Corn Pudding, Clapbacks, and Chaos

Thanksgiving in Evansville began with folding chairs, crock-pots, and **passive-aggressive whispers about parking.**

This year's gathering had one unspoken theme:
"Corn Pudding Showdown: The Revenge."

Because both **Aunt Debra** and **Cousin Kim** brought *their version* — again.

"Mine's the original," Debra said, placing hers on a hot plate with confidence.
"Mine's the one people actually eat," Kim replied, peeling back foil like she was unboxing a lawsuit.

Someone coughed.
Someone else whispered, "Round 3."

Meanwhile, **Grayson**, age 16 and a recent TikTok convert, was livestreaming everything.

"I'm just documenting," he said.
"For future trauma processing."

He caught:

- The moment Grandpa accidentally used whipped cream instead of mashed potatoes

- Uncle Brent asking *if turkey can be air-fried* without "compromising America"

- And a toddler yelling **"SHUSH!"** mid-grace when someone's phone went off.

That toddler?
Did not blink.

As the food hit the table, the corn pudding tension escalated.

Someone loudly asked *which one was which* — and Kim said:

"The fluffy one with flavor is mine. The dry one with regret belongs to Debra."

Debra didn't flinch.
She simply said,

"At least mine doesn't come from a box mix and delusion."

Grayson's phone vibrated violently.
Viewers were begging for a poll.

The green bean casserole had two layers of fried onions and **zero boundaries.**
The ham had been glazed *twice.*
And someone — no one would admit who — had put raisins in the stuffing.

A silent rage rippled through the room.
Even the rolls went cold.

Dessert brought temporary peace — until Uncle Larry tried to tell his *"classic"* Thanksgiving joke about corn and colon health.

No one laughed.
Not even Grandma.
She just said:

"Larry, you've had 74 Thanksgivings. Try silence."

Grayson's livestream hit 12,000 views.
He got a brand deal with a sparkling water company the next day.
The toddler is now feared like a tiny judge.

In Indiana, Thanksgiving is corn-fed, casserole-covered, and *one sentence away from petty.*
Show up with shade, and you'll leave with leftovers and a lesson.

15

❧

Iowa — Pies, Pitchforks, and a Pasture Situation

Thanksgiving in Ames was peaceful for exactly **43 minutes.**
The table was set.
The pies were cooling.
And the folding chairs were strategically placed to avoid last year's *potato spill incident.*

Then Cousin Bo showed up.
With the neighbors.
And the neighbor's parents.
And their dog.

"We just figured y'all'd have room," he said, already scooping mashed potatoes.

Grandma Mavis blinked twice.

"We set the table for *twelve*, not all of Polk County."

While everyone tried to play nice, **disaster struck.**

The pasture gate had been *left open.*
Bo's youngest, Cody, "just wanted to pet something with hooves."

Suddenly, the backyard was full of:

- 3 cows

- 1 confused turkey

- And Uncle Leonard chasing them in socks, yelling *"NO-BODY PANIC BUT GET THE CORN!"*

Inside, **the pie war began.**

Grandma Mavis makes the best pecan pie in six counties.
Everyone knows this.
So when Bo's *plus-one* Stacey (who no one had ever met) placed **her** pecan pie on the dessert table and said,

"Mine's keto-friendly!"

...things got frosty.
Frostier than the Cool Whip she brought in a reusable hummus container.

By the time grace was said —
(which included an emergency prayer for "fence integrity" and

"emotional barriers")
— the food was lukewarm and the tension was *simmering*.

Stacey asked if her pie was *"too advanced for traditional palates."*
Grandma said,

"It's brave, I'll give it that."
And cut herself an extra slice of *her own* pie.

The cows were finally wrangled by Bo's nephew who lured them
with cornbread muffins.
The dog ate the keto pie and sat quietly for five minutes like he was
rethinking everything. Then   he threw up next to the deviled eggs
and walked away changed.
Uncle Leonard now refuses to wear socks to family events.

At sunset, people packed up quietly.
Bo asked if he could take leftovers.
Grandma Mavis handed him one Tupperware and said:

"Only the raisins-in-the-stuffing portion. Y'all brought that,
y'all finish it."

In Iowa, Thanksgiving is family, fields, and **frosted boundaries.**
Just remember: lock the gate, label the pies, and don't try to out-
bake Grandma unless you came with backup.

16

❦

Kansas — Talent Shows, Stuffing Lies, and Drama

Thanksgiving in Topeka was going well... until **Aunt Denise** stood up, clapped twice, and said:

"Alright y'all — time for the *Thanksgiving Talent Showcase!*"

Silence.

Forks froze.
Uncle Martin whispered, *"Again with this nonsense?"*

But it was too late.
Aunt Denise had a laminated signup sheet, a portable karaoke speaker, and **the authority of a woman who once ran for PTA president unopposed.**

First up: Cousin Taylor.
Age 7. Tap shoes.

Danced to *"Uptown Funk"* using nothing but turkey legs for drumsticks.

Second: Grandma Lois.
Recited original poetry titled: *"The Gravy Boat of Dreams."*
No one understood it, but everyone clapped nervously.
Twice.

Third: Cousin Bryce.
Tried to freestyle rap.
Rhymed "Pilgrim" with "film him."
The dog left the room.

Then **Grandpa Earl** took the floor.
With a **megaphone.**

"I brought this so everyone can *actually hear me this year!*"

No one had requested that.
He used it anyway.

His talent?

"A dramatic reading of the Declaration of Independence. With voices."

By the word *"tyranny,"* the stuffing began to bubble over.

Speaking of stuffing...

Uncle Maurice's stuffing was **suspiciously well-reviewed** this year.
People were raving.

"So moist!"
"Is that smoked paprika?"
"Tastes like something you'd eat in a restaurant... that serves bail money."

Turns out — Marty had secretly **bought it from a local diner.**
Passed it off as homemade.
And even **entered it into the family's Annual Dish Vote.**

Scandal.
Aunt Denise screamed "FRAUD!"
Grandpa Earl yelled "IMPEACH HIM!" through the megaphone.
The dog came back just to bark.

Dessert?
Cancelled.
The karaoke speaker was confiscated.
Someone found the leftover stuffing in a takeout box with "To-Go Marty" scribbled on it.

Grandma Lois said,

"Next year, we're doing sandwiches."

Everyone agreed.
Even the megaphone.

In Kansas, Thanksgiving can be heartfelt, wholesome... and *highly competitive.*

Come hungry. Come talented.

But leave your store-bought stuffing — and your stage fright — at the door.

17

Kentucky — Biscuits, Bourbon, and a Camo Bride

Thanksgiving in Bowling Green came with all the staples:

- Buttermilk biscuits

- Deep-fried turkey

- And **two uncles in a heated debate about whether chicken is "just as thankful"** as turkey.

"Chicken is an everyday bird," said Uncle Boyd.
"Turkey is ceremonial," replied Uncle Virgil, sipping bourbon from a flask labeled *"Not Water."*

Meanwhile, Cousin Lacey showed up late.
Wearing a full-length **camouflage wedding dress.**
Veil included.

Heels optional.
Energy? **Unmatched.**

"I just felt like being formal," she said.
"Also, we eloped last weekend at Bass Pro."

"In the parking lot," added her new husband, Randy. "They let us pose with a kayak."

The room blinked.

Aunt Faye whispered, *"So the rumors were true."*

Dinner began with **a bourbon blessing** delivered by Grandpa Tucker.
He raised a glass, cleared his throat, and said:

"May your turkey be juicy, your whiskey be warm, and your decisions not end in paternity tests. Amen."

Cousin Lacey sipped her soda in silence.
Everyone looked at Randy.
Randy looked at the door.

The food?
Incredible.

- Fried turkey that had to be cut with a chainsaw (that was not a metaphor)

- Collard greens with bacon

- Corn pudding with a warning label

- And a mystery casserole labeled *"Don't Ask, Just Trust"*

Uncle Virgil dumped gravy on everything like it was his emotional support sauce.
Someone made a bourbon-glazed ham and forgot the ham.

"It's just bourbon now," they said, sipping from the pan.

Drama struck at dessert when **Lacey's mom** asked if she planned to wear white to *"the real wedding."*

Lacey stood up.
Twirled.
Said:

"This *is* real. It was blessed by a man with three fishing licenses."

No one challenged her.
The silence was sweet.
Like the pecan pie... and the vengeance in her smile.

Randy asked if they could *replay their vows* from his phone.
Grandma took the phone.
Put it in the freezer.
Said, "Some things don't need to thaw."

In Kentucky, Thanksgiving comes fried, filled, and a little unfiltered.

Show up bold. Speak soft.

And if you bring a camo wedding dress... bring matching energy.

18

Louisiana — Holy Water, Ghosts, and Gumbo Fights

Thanksgiving in Baton Rouge wasn't built around turkey.
It was built around **gumbo.**
Seafood, sausage, chicken, one tiny crab still trying to escape —
everything went in the pot.

Uncle Jules stirred it like it was a witch's brew.
He said the secret was "a little sass, a little salt, and a splash of
Hennessy."
Aunt Rochelle said the secret was "prayer and not letting Jules
near the kitchen."

So. Off to a great start.

Meanwhile, **Cousin Destiny** had come back from her first semester at college *spiritually awakened* and wearing beads that
matched no known outfit.

"I'm an energy reader now," she announced.
"And this room has ancestral tension."

"It also has okra," Grandma replied. "Focus on your plate."

Dinner included:

- Gumbo

- Fried turkey

- Crawfish cornbread

- Cranberry sauce that Destiny tried to **Cajun-ize** by adding cayenne and "a whisper of ancestral fire"

One bite in, a five-year-old cried.
Two bites in, Uncle Thibodeaux asked for ice cream.
Three bites in, Grandma stood up and pulled out her **holy water spray bottle.**

"Y'all playing with dark flavors," she said, misting the table like she was blessing a haunted Airbnb.

As always, there was **the debate: gumbo before or after grace?**

Grandpa Ernest said *after.*
Uncle Jules said *"You snooze, you scoop."*

Destiny interrupted the grace to ask if they could "honor the spirits of the land."

Aunt Rochelle muttered, "The only spirits I honor are in this punch."

Mid-meal, **the lights flickered.**

Everyone gasped.

Grandma said it was the Lord.

Destiny said it was "a wandering ancestor."

Uncle Jules said it was the breaker, and left to "fix it with a flashlight and faith."

He returned 20 minutes later with a beer and no update.

Dessert was bread pudding, sweet potato pie, and a failed attempt at "vegan beignets" that tasted like *confusion and regret.*

Destiny tried to cleanse the table with sage.

Grandma replaced it with potpourri.

"We are not about to burn the curtains again."

In Louisiana, Thanksgiving is rich, spicy, and maybe slightly haunted.

Come with an appetite, leave with a story, and don't touch the cranberry sauce unless your soul is prepared.

19

Maine — Cold Weather, Colder Comments

Thanksgiving in Bar Harbor kicked off with snowfall, silence, and **tense smiles hidden under knit scarves.**

Aunt Sheila had one mission this year:
"Keep it simple."

So naturally, she made:

- Lobster stuffing

- Haddock chowder

- A side of tension no one admitted to

"I just wanted to bring some local flavor," she said sweetly. "Because apparently tradition isn't *tasty* enough anymore," whispered Cousin Barb, already stirring the mashed potatoes like they insulted her dog.

Then in walked **Seth** — Barb's ex.
Still invited because *"he's good with the driveway."*

And with him?
Chloe.
The new girlfriend.
Wearing a Canada Goose jacket, vegan boots, and an innocent smile that screamed *"I brought gluten-free gravy."*

She did.

Dinner was served at 2:00 p.m. sharp.

By 2:07, the temperature in the dining room had dropped five degrees — emotionally.
By 2:15, someone whispered *"I miss when we didn't have sides that sparkle."*

Chloe's gravy was described as "brave."
The haddock chowder was "not how Nana made it."
And the lobster stuffing?
Half the table refused to eat seafood on Thanksgiving out of principle.

"It's not a *crustacean holiday*," muttered Uncle Gene.
"It's about birds and boundaries."

Grace was led by Grandpa Walter, who simply said:

"Thanks for whatever this is."

Then passed the rolls like he was dealing poker.

At dessert, Barb dropped a bomb:

"I made the apple pie from scratch. With *traditional Maine apples*. Not store-bought ones flown in from California."

Chloe blinked.
Seth choked on Cool Whip.
Everyone pretended to chew harder.

When tensions peaked, Aunt Sheila suggested a "family snowball walk" to cool off.
They lasted eight minutes.

Barb threw the first snowball.
It hit Seth.
Chloe slipped and took out the mashed potatoes.

They all came back in like **nothing happened.**

Except the pie?
Suddenly all gone.
And no one could find Chloe's gravy.

In Maine, Thanksgiving comes with seafood, snowfall, and **surgical levels of side-eye.**

Say it with a smile, bury it under butter, and if all else fails — blame the weather.

20

Maryland — Crab Cakes and the Old Bay Uprising

Thanksgiving in Baltimore was going *fine...*
Until Aunt Rhonda walked in, put her purse on the table, and loudly announced:

"If it ain't got Old Bay, it ain't got my attention."

That was directed at **cousin Malik**, who brought *plain deviled eggs.*

PLAIN.
Like witness protection program plain.

Tensions were already simmering because this year's dinner was a *"fusion feast."*
Which meant:

- Turkey *and* crab cakes

- Mac and cheese *and* quinoa salad

- Sweet potato pie *next to* a "sugar-conscious cinnamon alternative bake" that looked... beige

Uncle Cedric whispered,

"I didn't survive 2023 to eat a cinnamon alternative."
And pulled a bottle of hot sauce from his coat pocket like a silent protest.

Then Aunt Rhonda started **commentating.**
Out loud.
To no one.
And everyone.

"Mmm... see, that's what happens when you use box cornbread. It crumbles under pressure. Just like Chantel's last relationship."

"That turkey looks dry. Like Malik's career since he stopped working for the city."

Malik blinked.
Chantel blinked.
Grandma took a sip of wine and said,

"Let her cook."

Grace was led by Cousin Clay, who had recently "found herself" at a wellness retreat in Annapolis.

She opened with:

"Let us give thanks to the Earth, our ancestors, and the frequencies that brought us here."

Uncle Cedric coughed *"hustle culture"* into his napkin.

Aunt Rhonda whispered,

"She done thanked the ancestors but not the person who bought the ham."

The big brawl broke out over **crab cakes.**

Cousin Darren made a batch with no Old Bay.
Claimed he was "exploring flavor autonomy."

Aunt Rhonda stood up, grabbed a paper plate, and announced:

"I'm taking my casserole and my claws and heading to Miss Celeste's. Y'all keep your bland ambitions."

The front door closed behind her like punctuation.

Dessert was strained.
The sugar-conscious cinnamon bake remained untouched.
The pie was devoured in silence.

Someone played Anita Baker.
Peace was declared... until Christmas.

   In Maryland, Thanksgiving is seasoned, saucy, and narrated in real time.
Come correct. Bring Old Bay.
And don't let your side dish become a subplot.

21

Massachusetts — The Great Gravy Reckoning

T hanksgiving in Salem (yes, *that* Salem) was already tense, and not just because of the witch trial jokes Cousin Danny refused to stop making.

"Y'all are lucky I made it out of last year alive," he grinned, passing the cranberry sauce.
"Grandma tried to burn me at the stake for bringing oat milk."

She did not laugh.
She also did not forget.

This year, things escalated *before* dinner even started when **Cousin Priya** set up a whiteboard titled:

"Decolonizing Thanksgiving: A Brief Family Guide"

Uncle Pete blinked.

"We just wanted pie, not a protest."

Priya came with handouts.
Grandma came with **gravy and side-eye.**

The table included:

- Stuffing with sausage

- Mashed potatoes with butter *and judgment*

- A separate, silently shamed *"plant-based corner"*

- And Priya's contribution:
a **seasonal heritage stew** that smelled like ambition and oregano

"This dish honors indigenous foodways," she explained.
"It also clears sinuses," muttered Danny.

Grace arrived late — and so did the Patriots metaphor.

"Great Uncle George raised his glass, nodded solemnly, and said, "May this meal be more consistent than our quarterback."

Priya added,

"And honor the land and those it belonged to before colonialism."

Grandma cleared her throat like a warning shot.
Uncle Pete blinked *extra hard.*

The real drama hit when **someone skipped the gravy.**

Grandma's gravy.

"I just didn't want to consume dairy," Priya said.
"Or oppression."

Silence.

Grandma put down her fork.
Stared across the table.

"This gravy has been passed down for three generations.
If oppression was involved, it was *delicious.*"

Dessert was a mix of apple pie, ancestral guilt, and two slices of
something that looked like pumpkin but tasted like a **bitter lesson.**

Danny suggested a family group therapy circle.
Uncle George turned up the TV.
Priya offered to smudge the living room.
Someone unplugged the diffuser.

In Massachusetts, Thanksgiving is historical, hysterical, and full
of *very calm arguments said through clenched teeth.*
If you want peace at the table, bring gravy.
And don't touch the whiteboard.

22

Michigan — Fiancé Drama and the U.P. Confusion

Thanksgiving in Grand Rapids was rolling smooth:
The kids were building snow turkeys.
The adults were building up *emotional walls*.
And Aunt Deb had *already* claimed credit for the stuffing, even though she only brought napkins.

Then **Cousin Jared** walked in.
With **Amélie**.

"She's from Montreal," he announced proudly.
"We're engaged."

Silence.
Aunt Deb blinked.
Uncle Joe coughed into his Vernors.

Amélie wore a red coat, a polite smile, and the emotional confidence of someone who thought **Michigan was still part of Canada.**

"This is my first American Thanksgiving," she beamed.
"I read it involves... cheese? And... aggressive prayer?"

The table held **seven casseroles**, including:

- Green bean (classic)

- Sweet potato with marshmallows (childlike)

- Tuna surprise (no one claimed it)

- A vegan "Detroit spice bake" that smelled like gym socks

- And Amélie's "Quebecois root vegetable dream," which someone described as *"hot sadness in a pan."*

Jared took two servings.
No one else made eye contact.

Then came **The U.P. Debate.**

It started innocently:

"Amélie, are you excited to explore Michigan?"
She replied,
"We're heading north tomorrow. Jared says we'll drive through the Upper... um... what's it called?"

Uncle Joe jumped in like it was *Jeopardy*:

"**Upper Peninsula.** Or *God's Country.*"

Aunt Deb added,

"But it's not *real* Michigan. You need a passport and snow tires to get there."

This ignited a **twenty-minute, emotionally-charged geography brawl** featuring hand gestures, references to lake borders, and three printouts from Wikipedia.

Amélie just blinked.

"I thought we were going to see deer."

Grace was delivered by Grandpa Lou, who included:

- Gratitude for snow tires

- A subtle dig at Jared for "never calling"

- And the phrase: *"Lord, help this Canadian understand our family before she legally enters it."*

Amélie smiled.
Took a polite bite of every casserole.
Declared them "interesting."

Dessert was wet apple crisp.
Amélie said it reminded her of **"a sad orchard."**
Grandma said,

"Well, Jared's last girlfriend didn't cry about fruit."

In Michigan, Thanksgiving is cold, casserole-covered, and *culturally informative.*
Bring layers. Bring backup gravy.
And if you're introducing a mystery fiancé, maybe wait 'til Easter.

23

Minnesota — Hotdish, Ice Smiles, and Post-it Shade

Thanksgiving in St. Paul started with snow flurries and silent resentment.
The good kind.
The kind where people smile through their teeth and say *"Interesting choice!"* like it's a dagger in a parka.

Aunt Linda hosted.
Aunt Karen *thought* she was co-hosting.
Neither confirmed anything... but both brought table centerpieces, *and* passive-aggressively claimed "the good deviled eggs."

"Oh, did I not say I was bringing them? Huh. Must've slipped my mind like someone's RSVP."

The **hotdish buffet** included:

- Tater tot hotdish (classic)

- Tuna noodle hotdish (controversial)

- A mysterious one labeled *"Gluten-curious"*

- And of course, **Jell-O salad** with suspended grapes, marshmallows, and trauma

Uncle Erik called it *"midwestern ceviche."*
No one laughed.
He's still proud.

Trouble started around **Post-it Note Number One.**

A yellow sticky appeared on the cranberry mold:

"Not tart *enough.* :) —Anonymous"

Then another on Karen's bundt cake:

"Little dry, but brave effort. ;)"

By the time grace was said, the rolls had *three notes*, and someone had put one directly on the fridge:

"FYI: This is not where leftovers go. Please consult previous years."

No one owned up.
Everyone blamed Linda.
She blamed the Holy Spirit.

Grace was led by Cousin Brayden, age 12, who simply said:

"Thank you, God, for keeping us from saying what we're all thinking."

Grandpa said *"Amen"* before he even finished.

Dessert included:

- Pumpkin pie

- Rice pudding (questionable)

- Lefse (no one under 40 ate it)

- And a *"Scandinavian Surprise"* brought by a coworker no one remembered inviting

They smiled.
They ate.
They texted each other from across the table.

"Who brought Russ??"
"He's with Jan."
"Who's Jan??"
"Exactly."

At clean-up, Karen and Linda finally spoke directly to each other.

"Next year, maybe I'll host."
"Next year, maybe *no one* will."

Grandma stood up and said,

"Next year, we're doing lasagna and silence."

Everyone clapped.
Except Russ.
Who was still eating the rice pudding.

In Minnesota, Thanksgiving is 35% food, 65% internalized tension, and 100% served with a smile.
If you feel judged, you probably are.
And if you leave a Post-it... *sign it, coward.* :)

24

Mississippi — Cornbread Wars and Sweet Tea Shade

Thanksgiving in Jackson started with gospel music in the background, gravy on the stove, and **Miss Gladys declaring war through a pan of cornbread.**

"I made mine the way my *mama* taught me."

"And I made mine the way people *like it*," replied Cousin Monique, with a smile so tight it could slice yam.

They both brought cast iron skillets.
They both said *"try mine first."*
And the family *immediately* knew:
This would not be a peaceful meal.

The menu was full Southern Thanksgiving glory:

- Turkey *and* ham

- Mac & cheese baked until the top crust crunched like judgment

- Greens with turkey necks

- Sweet potatoes so sweet your dentist could hear them

And two full pans of cornbread with **completely different energies.**

The taste test showdown?
Immediate.
And vicious.

Uncle Big Reggie took a bite of Gladys's, paused, and said:

"This tastes like tradition."
Then bit Monique's and added:
"And this one tastes like **progress.**"

Wrong answer.
Monique stood up.
Gladys smoothed her napkin with trembling fingers.
Grandma put her Bible down.
The gospel music got louder *on its own.*

Grace was **interrupted** twice:

- Once by someone's phone ringtone (*"Knuck If You Buck"*)

- And once by Aunt Cookie yelling "WHO TOOK THE LAST NECKBONE!?"

Both were forgiven.
Eventually.

Dessert brought **more drama**.

Monique made sweet potato pie with a brûléed top.
Miss Gladys said,

"We don't set fire to our desserts."
Monique replied,
"Only the ones that need resurrection."

Uncle Big Reggie tried both pies.
Said nothing.
Took a nap.

The evening ended with:

- A dominoes game that nearly caused a family split

- Three "bless your hearts" that definitely weren't blessings

- And Miss Gladys slipping Monique a *sticky note inside a Tupperware* that said:

"It was too moist. Next year, just bring napkins."

In Mississippi, Thanksgiving isn't just a meal — it's a **culinary duel wrapped in Bible verses and butter.**
If you come for the cornbread, you better *bring your ancestors with you.*

25

Missouri — Monopoly Fights and the Missing Pie

Thanksgiving in St. Louis started like it always does:

- One folding table too short

- One cousin too dramatic

- And **four types of pie** ranked unofficially but passionately

This year's host, Aunt Beverly, ran things *military-style*.
Assigned seating. Strict prayer time.
And a printed chart labeled **"Potluck Expectations vs. Historical Performance."**

Uncle Chuck blinked.

"Why is there a bar graph?"
Beverly:
"Some of y'all needed feedback."

The menu:

- Turkey (smoked and talked about like it had feelings)

- Cheesy broccoli rice casserole (bubbled with judgment)

- Mac & cheese that sparked whispers of "who made THIS batch?"

- And of course... the pies.

Except one.
Grandma Evelyn's famous **chocolate chess pie?**
Gone.

Missing.
Not sliced. Not touched.
Just vanished like an ex who still owes you $60.

"I placed it right here," Grandma said, eyes scanning the room like a detective in a Lifetime movie.
"On this embroidered runner. Next to my dignity."

Tension rose during the **Annual Monopoly Game**, which had been banned twice and resurrected out of tradition and spite.

Cousin Marcus made it five minutes before flipping the board.
Blamed "a toxic capitalist structure."
Also claimed someone stole his $500s.

Uncle Darrell called him *soft*.
Marcus called him *mortgaged emotionally*.

Then Cousin Nia stood up to file an official complaint.
About her seat.

She handed Aunt Beverly a literal piece of paper titled:

Folding Chair Grievance Form — Year 3
Stated her back "deserved better" and included diagrams.

Aunt Beverly ignored her.
Grandma whispered, *"Maybe that's where the pie went — into her ego."*

Dessert was pure tension and half-sincere compliments.
"Interesting crust."
"Very... bold raisins."
"I liked the texture, I just didn't like the taste."

Someone slipped a sticky note on the fridge that read:

"Y'all don't deserve Grandma's pie anyway."

At cleanup, the chess pie was found.
Under the Monopoly board.
Untouched. Cold. Full of betrayal.

Grandma looked at it.
Looked at Marcus.
Said nothing.
Took the whole pie home.

In Missouri, Thanksgiving is full of rules, rivalries, and **unexpected disappearances.**
Play nice. Sit upright.
And if you want pie? Guard it like your reputation.

26

Montana — Horses, Hemp Rolls, and a Pinecone Vow

Thanksgiving in Billings was supposed to be lowkey.
Just family.
Just food.
Just peaceful vibes with a backdrop of open sky and *mildly suppressed emotions.*

Then **Cousin Skylar** rolled in.
On an actual **horse.**
With a guitar, a hemp tote bag, and **Harper**, her new "life partner-slash-wilderness therapist."

"We met at a silent retreat near Glacier," Skylar said.
"We've already done three past life regressions together."

Grandma just said,

"You couldn't have just brought rolls?"

The menu was a mix of classics and *question marks*:

- Roasted turkey with herbs (and actual feathers still on the porch)

- Elk meatballs from someone's freezer

- Mashed potatoes "reimagined" with almond milk

- Hemp dinner rolls that tasted like notebook paper and grass

"They're anti-inflammatory," Harper offered.
Uncle Carl said,
"So is silence."

Grace was led by Skylar and included:

- A quote from Rumi

- A moment of breathwork

- And a brief **chant for digestive clarity**

Aunt Darlene coughed and said,

"Let the Lord handle the roughage."

During dinner, Harper shared that they "don't believe in traditional marriage," but had **technically eloped** two days ago by **exchanging pinecones under a waterfall.**

"It felt real," Skylar said, tearing up.
"And we signed a mushroom cap as our certificate."

No one made eye contact.
Grandma added,

"Still no rolls, huh?"

The drama peaked when **Harper tried to lead a post-meal drum circle.**
They brought two hand drums and a single tuning fork.

Uncle Carl countered by playing *"Sweet Home Alabama"* on a Bluetooth speaker and refusing to acknowledge any beat not in 4/4 time.

Dessert was a mix of:

- Huckleberry pie

- Vegan "bliss squares" that tasted like disappointment

- And Skylar's *raw gratitude fudge,* which gave one kid a nosebleed

"It's the detox," Harper said.
"Or the altitude," someone whispered.

As the sun set, Skylar packed up half the stuffing and one of Grandma's antique serving spoons.

Grandma yelled,

"BRING MY SPOON BACK OR I'M PRAYING FOR YOUR MARRIAGE TO GET TAXED."

Skylar waved from horseback.
Harper bowed.
The horse neighed like it, too, was spiritually confused.

In Montana, Thanksgiving is wild, weird, and occasionally **hoof-delivered.**
Respect the land, pass the meatballs,
and if you bring tuning forks, *bring cornbread too.*

27

❧

Nebraska — Frozen Pies, Camo, and Football Grace

Thanksgiving in Lincoln was supposed to kick off at 2 p.m.

But **kickoff on TV** happened at 1:30.
So naturally, **Uncle Dean** parked himself in front of the flatscreen with a turkey leg and declared:

"The Lord understands. He made football too."

Grace?
Skipped.
Postponed.
Rescheduled between the first and second quarter.

Grandma **did not approve.**
She pulled the plug mid-replay.
The room gasped.
Uncle Dean whispered, *"This is persecution."*

The house was full of:

- Kids hopped up on Kool-Aid

- Teen cousins making TikToks in the garage

- Aunt Phyllis wearing a full **camo jacket** and claiming she'd "been out scouting ducks" ten minutes ago

"The casserole's still warm. So am I," she said, sitting down with binoculars still around her neck.

Then came **The Frozen Pie Incident™**.

Uncle Matt brought **store-bought pecan pies** — frozen, in-box, with the sticker still on.

He handed them to Cousin Emily and said:

"You got a microwave, right?"

A microwave. For pies.
The room stiffened like undercooked stuffing.

Emily, who had **been up since 5 a.m. baking**, turned so red the Cool Whip curdled.

"You really brought Walmart to my walnut crust?" she asked. "Those pies don't even have a *soul*."

Tension exploded at grace, which finally happened **during half-time.**

Grandma started to pray.
Uncle Dean tried to sneak in earbuds.
Someone said, *"Turn down the crockpot, I can't hear the Lord."*

Then **a child let out a full scream** because the mac and cheese had crispy bits.

"I want the *soft* kind!"
"We're all dealing with disappointment," whispered Aunt Phyllis.

Dessert was served with side-eyes and vengeance.

No one touched Matt's pie.
Matt's pie sat there like a dare no one accepted. Even the flies hesitated.

Emily's pie?
Gone in five minutes.
She labeled the empty dish *"Baked, Not Bought"* and slid it in front of Matt.

In Nebraska, Thanksgiving is a game of family, football, and **frozen mistakes.**
Microwave if you must, but don't microwave your credibility.

28

Nevada — Buffets, Bluffs, and Thanksgiving Bets

T hanksgiving in Las Vegas was held at Aunt Val's this year — a woman who believes in:

- **Sequins at all meals**

- **A BYOB (Bring Your Own Butter) policy**

- And **buffet-style serving "for drama control."**

"Let them plate their own bad decisions," she said, placing plastic labels next to every dish.

The menu had range:

- Turkey (carved live on TikTok)

- Ham (with a cinnamon glaze and glitter)

- Mashed potatoes (in chafing dishes from a hotel auction)

- And **mystery cranberry shots in Solo cups**

"Is it juice?"
"Is it vodka?"
"Yes."

Enter **Cousin Blake**, who brought **a date named Sapphire** (her legal name).
No one had heard of her.
She brought two things:

1. A fruit tray

2. A **deck of custom Uno cards** with real gold edges

"We thought we'd raise the stakes this year," Blake said.
"Winner gets first pick of leftovers."

WHAT.

The Uno game popped off immediately.
By the third round:

- Uncle Tony had gone all in on sweet potato pie

- Grandma had folded emotionally

- Sapphire had Reverse-Reversed the whole table into a passive-aggressive silence

Someone whispered, *"This is how we lost Thanksgiving '07."*

Meanwhile, the buffet turned into a **strategic negotiation zone.**

"I'll swap you a drumstick for a scoop of Aunt Val's green bean casserole."
"Only if you throw in an extra roll. I know what those things are worth."

A toddler tried to stack three slices of pie.
Blake told him, "Play to win, little man."

The toddler nodded like a legend and added Cool Whip.

Grace was delivered by Aunt Val herself, holding a champagne flute and one heel in her hand.

"Lord, thank you for this meal, this family, and the fact that I haven't slapped anyone today — even though I was tested."

Amen.

Dessert became chaos.

Cousin Blake bet Sapphire's banana pudding in a final Uno hand.

He lost.
Sapphire stood up, took her tray, and said:

"I'm taking my pudding and my power back."

She left to a standing ovation.
Someone tossed confetti made of napkin shreds.

In Nevada, Thanksgiving isn't just dinner — it's a game.
Bring your plate, bring your strategy, and don't bluff if your pie can't back it up.

29

New Hampshire — Where Pie Beats Policy

Thanksgiving in Concord began with frost on the driveway, cider on the stove, and **Gary's campaign signs... in the living room.**

Yes. **Cousin Gary.**
Running for **Ward 6 City Council** like his life — and this mashed potato bowl — depended on it.

"Thanksgiving's about giving thanks *and* engaging the community," he said, taping a QR code to the butter dish.

Aunt Trudy had organized the meal **potluck style**, which was immediately complicated by:

- **No official assignments**

- **Three kinds of stuffing**

- **Zero vegetables unless you count pickled onions**

- And Gary labeling his cranberry sauce as *"Locally-Made by a Future Leader"*

Someone muttered, *"So was Nixon."*

Dinner began with polite bickering over:

- Gary's yard sign centerpiece

- Whether apple pie was more American than pumpkin

- And whether **Gary's ex-wife should've been invited**

She was.
She brought the best rolls.
Also, a date named Kevin who *just happened* to work in voter registration.

Gary dropped his fork.
Grandma passed him wine.

Grace was delivered by Aunt Trudy —
Simple.
Classic.
Until Gary interrupted to say,

"And let's remember the importance of civic engagement—"

Uncle Lenny cut him off with:

"Let's remember to *eat*, Gary. And *campaign after dessert*."

Things escalated during dessert.

Gary passed out **custom pie plates** with his slogan:
"A Slice of Progress for Ward 6"
And then tried to give a toast.

"To transparency, tradition, and this maple-glazed carrot cake,
which, by the way, I personally—"

"Gary, sit down," said Grandma.
"You're about to get voted out of this family."

As the pie dwindled, Kevin leaned over to Gary and said,

"I'd vote for your ex before I vote for you."
Then took the last piece of carrot cake.

Gary stood up.
Walked out.
Took his signs with him.

The cranberry sauce was left behind.
Untouched.
Unloved.

In New Hampshire, Thanksgiving is about family, food, and *fierce, off-cycle elections.*

If you want votes, don't campaign with cranberry.

And if Grandma's still hosting, know when to yield the floor.

30

New Jersey — Gravy Fights and Stuffing Shade

Thanksgiving in Hoboken was already running an hour behind schedule —
Because Lucia wouldn't sit down until the gravy had "cooked long enough to earn respect."

(And yes, it's **gravy,** not "sauce." That debate? Still ongoing. Still violent.)

The table was a mash-up of:

- Turkey

- Lasagna

- Meatballs

- Antipasti tray the size of a small mattress

- And **Cousin Nico's "elevated take on stuffing"** that involved quinoa, pine nuts, and disrespect

"It's Thanksgiving, not Coachella," Uncle Sal whispered.

Nico wore a turtleneck and *smugness*.
He called his dish **"deconstructed"** and brought his own spoon.
Uncle Sal brought a bad attitude and **brass knuckles made of sarcasm.**

Grace was delivered by Aunt Gina — short, sweet, and punctuated by three side-eyes and a *"We forgive but don't forget."*

Everyone nodded.
Everyone knew.

Dinner was loud.
Louder than the football game.
Louder than the espresso machine.
Louder than Grandma yelling *"Don't you DARE put ketchup on that meat!"*

Then it happened.
The bread basket flip.

Cousin Franca, fresh off her third mimosa, asked:

"So, are we gonna pretend Aunt Angela's stuffing isn't dry every year?"

Boom.

Bread rolls flew.
Someone gasped.
Someone else clapped.

Angela stood up, knocked over a sippy cup, and said:

"I've been holding back since 2015. But not today."

Dessert was served with **tension, tiramisu, and tiny paper plates that couldn't hold the weight of the family drama.**

Someone brought cannoli.
Someone else brought store-bought cookies.
Grandma made eye contact and said:

"This is why I pray for all of you."

Nico left early.
Angela left loudly.
Franca left with two containers of meatballs and zero shame.

In New Jersey, Thanksgiving is love, yelling, and a little lasagna in every corner of the fridge.
Don't come empty-handed.
And don't deconstruct the stuffing unless you're ready to reconstruct your relationship.

31

New Mexico — Flan Fights and Chile-Spiced Drama

T hanksgiving in Santa Fe started out chill — like most things in the desert do.

The table was set outside, framed by adobe walls and judgment-free vibes... *so far.*

Aunt Lourdes brought **turkey spiced with green chile and roasted over mesquite.**
It smelled like heaven.
It tasted like **justice.**

Then **Cousin Mateo** arrived...
Wearing a turtleneck.
Carrying a **glass dish covered in foil and pride.**

"I replaced the pumpkin pie this year," he said.
"With flan. It's more culturally connected."

Dead. Silence.
Even the wind paused.

"Pumpkin pie is sacred," whispered Tía Yvette.
"Even the pilgrims would be mad."

Abuela slowly removed her apron.
Set it on the table.
Then simply said:

"You better back that custard up."

The meal went on:

- Stuffing with hatch chile and chorizo

- Tamales with turkey instead of pork (controversial but tolerated)

- Cornbread that could double as a pillow

- And cranberry sauce "infused with ancestral intention" (whatever that meant — it came in a jar)

Grace was led by Uncle Luis, who included:

- A prayer for family unity

- A prayer for digestive strength

- And a prayer for **"whoever brought flan without community input."**

Mateo clinked his spoon on a wine glass and began a speech about "decolonizing dessert."
He got two words in before Abuela stood up and said,

"Do you even own a pie plate?"

Later, during dessert:

- The flan slid off the dish

- The table tilted

- The dog licked it

- And Abuela handed out **emergency slices of frozen pumpkin pie from last year**

Everyone cheered.
Someone said, "She's always got it like that."
She nodded.

"Because I planned for this betrayal."

Mateo was last seen leaving with the flan in a cooler labeled "For Work."

No one said goodbye.

No one asked for the recipe.

In New Mexico, Thanksgiving is hot, heartfelt, and not for amateurs.

If you're bringing flan, bring backup.

And maybe don't mess with the pie unless your Abuela signs off — *in writing.*

32

New York — Phones Down, Bread Hidden, Drama Up

Thanksgiving in Brooklyn was *supposed* to be chic.

Cousin Amber was hosting for the first time, and she sent out **a very aggressive group email** titled:

"This Year, We're Doing Things Differently: A Mindful Thanksgiving"

Rules included:

- No phones at the table

- No gluten

- No yelling

- No shoes in the apartment

- And no "uninvited emotional energy"

Uncle Lionel responded with,

"I'm still bringing cornbread and complaints."

Guests arrived to a minimalist table, a scented candle labeled *"Calm Presence,"* and a playlist called **"Gratitude Vibes Only."**

Then walked in **Cousin Frankie** — holding a box of Popeyes, wearing Jordans, and FaceTiming someone named "Peaches" the whole time.

"Yo, they got quinoa stuffing," he told his screen.
"I ain't mad, just confused."

Amber's turkey?
Brined, basted, and **bland**.

The gluten-free rolls were *emotionally dry.*
The mushroom gravy was described as *"brave."*
And the kale salad was *"less of a dish and more of a dare."*

Aunt Paulette pulled out her own bottle of ranch.
Said nothing.
Poured freely.

Grace began with a sound bowl chime.

Amber whispered,

"Let's go around and each say what we're releasing this year."

Uncle Lionel said,

"I'm releasing the memory of this stuffing."
Frankie said,
"I'm releasing Peaches' cousin for being messy."
Peaches (still on FaceTime):
"Don't bring me into y'all's spiritual process."

Mid-meal, a shout came from the kitchen.
Grandma had found gluten.

Specifically:
A bag of King's Hawaiian rolls in the pantry.
Unopened.
Hidden.
Contraband.

"Someone brought backup bread," she said, holding it like evidence.
"Ain't nobody trusting that flax sponge."

Dessert was... a struggle.
Amber served **a cashew-based pumpkin cheesecake** that tasted like *intentions*.

Frankie pulled out a slice of Junior's cheesecake he'd kept in his backpack.

Peaches clapped from the phone.

Grandma took a bite and said,

"See? This is what forgiveness tastes like."

In New York, Thanksgiving is about food, family, and **fighting the urge to text through it all.**

You can ban gluten. You can ban phones.

But you can't ban *New York-level honesty* — not even with a scented candle.

33

North Carolina — Mac, Marriage, and Collard Chaos

Thanksgiving in Raleigh kicked off with the usual:

- A long table that barely fit the living room

- An even longer side-eye from Grandma when *unsweet tea* showed up

- And a playlist alternating between gospel and Fantasia

Then **Terrence** stood up during grace.
Yes — **during grace.**

"While we're giving thanks... I just wanna say I'm thankful for this woman beside me—"

Gasps. Chokes. Forks dropping.

Aunt Carolyn pressed a hand to her chest like she was physically holding her heart in place.
Uncle Mo hit pause on the gravy pour.

Terrence got down on one knee.
In front of the yams.

"Marcia, will you—"

"SIT DOWN," Grandma said, still praying.
"The Lord is not done, and neither are these biscuits."

Proposal postponed.
Turkey served.
Tension... **marinated.**

The spread:

- Fried turkey, crispy and righteous

- Dressing so dense it had its own gravity

- Sweet potatoes with toasted pecans *and* a whisper of bourbon

- Mac and cheese that made three people moan out loud

Then came **the greens.**

Collard Gate.

Cousin Shayla — fresh from a vegan soul food blog — said she'd made the greens "lighter" this year.

Lighter = **coconut oil.**

COCONUT. OIL.

Uncle Mo took one bite and whispered,

"Who gave the greens a tan?"

Aunt Carolyn stood up mid-chew.

"You did what to my mother's recipe?"
"It's heart healthy!" Shayla protested.
"So is minding your business," said Grandma.

Half the table passed the coconut collards to the dog. The dog took a sniff and walked off offended.

Dessert brought peace.
Until Terrence tried **again.**

"Now that we're all full—"
"We were full *before*," said Marcia, side-eye sharp.
"You gonna propose *after* I ate two plates of turkey?"

Grandma nodded.

"No woman wants to start her forever while bloated."

Terrence sat down.
Someone passed him pie.
It was silent.

Except the sound of his ring being quietly zipped back into his coat.

In North Carolina, Thanksgiving is bold, buttered, and best served with **boundaries.**
Don't mess with the mac.
Don't fix greens that aren't broken.
And if you're proposing? Wait 'til *after* dessert — *and maybe next year.*

34

North Dakota — Where Feelings Go to Hibernate

Thanksgiving in Bismarck started with **three feet of snow** and **zero visible emotion.**

Grandma had already cooked everything by 7 a.m.
The turkey was ready.
The sides were labeled.
The family?
Emotionally snowed in.

Uncle Don walked in, dusted off his boots, and said:

"Guess we made it."

Aunt Carla nodded.
"Mmhmm. Lotta snow."
"Yep."

"Stuffing's on the counter."
"Solid."

This was **a full emotional exchange.**
No one needed to say more.
No one would.

The menu:

- Turkey (dry but respected)

- Mashed potatoes (served with no butter explanation — just butter)

- Jell-O salad (with floating fruit and *confusion*)

- Stuffing that weighed more than a snow shovel

Cousin Mark took one bite and whispered,

"This'll keep you warm in a blizzard."

Uncle Don replied,

"That's the goal."

Grace was led by Grandpa Herb.
He said:

"We're here. Let's eat."
And everyone nodded like it was Scripture.

Mid-meal, **Cousin Bri tried to talk about her feelings.**
Said she was "processing things."

Silence.

Grandma refilled the gravy.
Aunt Carla said,

"Processing? You a computer now?"
And then asked someone to pass the cranberries.

The drama?
Came from **a green bean casserole standoff.**

There were **two.**
One classic.
One "lightened up" version made by Cousin Joel, who'd "read a blog."

People took the classic.
No one touched Joel's.

He offered it three times.
Eventually just **put it in the garage.**
Didn't say a word.
Took a walk in the snow.

He came back with icicles on his mustache.
Still said nothing.

Dessert included:

- Store-bought pie that no one admitted buying

- Cool Whip still in the tub

- And a casual whisper: *"We don't talk politics at this table."*

No one even brought it up.
But they still said it.
Because tradition.

In North Dakota, Thanksgiving is quiet, heavy, and **best served with wool socks and emotional restraint.**
If someone says "It's fine," it's not.
But don't ask. Just pass the pie.

35

Ohio — Buckeyes, Trivia Night, and Casserole Wars

Thanksgiving in Columbus kicked off with a family group text that read:

"We will NOT be turning off the game for grace this year." — **Uncle Ted**

No one replied.
Because everyone agreed.

Ohio State was playing.
Grandpa had on his jersey.
The turkey was still resting, but **the fandom was on fire.**

The table was pure Midwest:

- Turkey

- Mashed potatoes with "a touch" of mayonnaise (don't ask)

- Buckeye candies made by someone's kid with *way too much* peanut butter

- And the annual **Layered Casserole Cold War**

That's right.
Two cousins.
One kitchen.
Two *completely different* seven-layer casseroles.

Cousin Jamie called hers "classic, crowd-tested."
Cousin Neil called his "innovative."
One included kale. The other included rage.

Half the room took both and just prayed silently.
The other half made direct eye contact while chewing.

Then came the **unsanctioned trivia game.**

Aunt Janet, recently retired and very enthusiastic about "enriching traditions," stood up after dinner and yelled:

"It's time for THANKSGIVING FAMILY TRIVIA NIGHT!"

Groans.
Real ones.
Uncle Ted pretended to fall asleep.

"First question," she said, "What year was the first Macy's Thanksgiving Parade?"

Someone shouted *"Irrelevant!"*
Someone else whispered, *"I came here to eat, not earn badges."*

During round two, **Grandpa Brad buzzed in by yelling "1982!"** for every answer, regardless of the question.

Even the toddler got a point.

Aunt Janet insisted it built *"emotional bonds."*
Uncle Ted suggested **cornhole** instead.
Grandpa yelled *"1982!"* again for effect.

Dessert brought momentary peace:

- Pumpkin pie

- Apple pie

- Store-bought cheesecake that no one admitted buying

- And one *"raw banana oat slice"* that was quietly returned to the kitchen like a library book no one wanted

Trivia ended when someone accidentally knocked the game cards into the gravy boat.
Aunt Janet took it as divine intervention.

Grandpa got a touchdown alert.
Everyone clapped.
Someone passed him another Buckeye candy like a trophy.

In Ohio, Thanksgiving is food, football, and **forced fun if you're not quick enough to hide.**
Just say "1982," and pass the Buckeyes.
Everything else is optional.

36

Oklahoma — Boots,
Blowouts, and Turkey
Trouble

Thanksgiving in Tulsa kicked off with **a propane tank, a turkey on a hook, and a cousin named J.T. wearing cowboy boots and zero fear.**

"We fryin' it like Grandpa did," J.T. said, dunking the turkey into **scorching oil** like it owed him money.

Grandma yelled from the porch:

"Just don't set the driveway on fire *again!*"

J.T. winked.
The turkey sizzled.
The wind howled like a warning.

Inside, **Aunt Peggy** was setting the table while yelling over the weather:

"Tie down the pie table! Last year we lost a coconut cream to the fence line!"

Uncle Chet hammered a pie tin into the table with a butter knife.
Someone else muttered, *"Only in Oklahoma."*

The menu was southern-style survival food:

- Deep-fried turkey

- Corn casserole so thick it needed a permit

- Deviled eggs with jalapeños *and judgment*

- Biscuits made with bacon grease and love

But someone (we won't name names, *Tiffany*) brought **a tofu loaf.**
Wrapped in aluminum.
Announced it like a TED Talk.

"It's protein-forward and environmentally respectful."
J.T. said, *"It looks like wet insulation."*

Grace was led by **Grandpa Beau**, wearing a bolo tie and holding a Styrofoam cup.

"We thank the Lord, the land, and whoever made these mashed potatoes that slapped me straight to heaven."

Someone yelled **"YEEHAW"** halfway through.
No one knows why.
No one objected.

Drama blew in with the wind.

Literally.

A gust hit mid-meal.
Napkins flew.
The Jell-O salad hit the deck.
And **Tiffany's tofu loaf** was last seen tumbling toward the neighbor's truck bed.

"Don't chase it!" someone yelled.
"Let nature decide!"

Dessert was sweet, chaotic, and lightly dusted in driveway grit.

The coconut cream pie?
Saved.
The tofu?
Gone.

Grandma said,

"That wind's got taste."

In Oklahoma, Thanksgiving is windy, wild, and **deep-fried to perfection or catastrophe.**
Strap down your pies.
Trust your boots.
And if someone yells "Yeehaw," just go with it.

37

Oregon — Foraged Feelings
and the Loaf of Regret

Thanksgiving in Portland began with **rain, flannel, and a group agreement to "honor all diets, traumas, and seasonal allergies."**

The turkey was locally raised.
The kale had a backstory.
The playlist was soft banjo covers of '90s hip-hop.

And **Cousin Rain** (born Jessica, now Rain) showed up with **a mushroom-based entrée called "Closure."**

"It's a fermented wild-foraged mushroom loaf inspired by my breakup with Jordan."
"The accountant?" someone asked.
"No, the ukulele instructor."

The table included:

- Quinoa stuffing

- Vegan gravy (the texture of deep apology)

- Root vegetables "blessed by moonlight"

- And one poor soul who asked if there was "just regular butter?"

Everyone stared.
Aunt Phoebe passed him a pamphlet.
It said, *"Let's Talk About Cow Trauma."*

Grace was led by **Uncle Jasper**, who opened a mason jar of essential oils and said:

"Let's breathe through our expectations."

Someone lit sage.
Someone else sneezed.
Rain added, *"And let us not force reconciliation upon dishes not ready to be digested."*

Grandma blinked.
Reached for the wine.

Drama brewed in the **Dessert Discussion Circle.**

Rain announced that the traditional pies had been replaced by:

- Cashew pumpkin mousse

- Maple-kissed squash pudding

- And a freeform poetry reading titled *"I Am the Pie I Needed."*

Uncle Bo brought a Costco pie anyway.
Kept it in the trunk.
Served slices in the garage like a bootleg pastry dealer.

"Don't tell Rain," he whispered, handing out plates.
"This one has crust. And sugar. And joy."

Later, the mushroom loaf was left mostly untouched.
Rain said, *"It's okay. Not everyone's ready to process grief with their taste buds."*

Grandma clapped.

"Then stop putting it on the buffet."

In Oregon, Thanksgiving is thoughtful, therapeutic, and occasionally fungus-forward.
Honor your healing.
Bring your own pie.
And if you name a side dish after an ex, *don't expect seconds.*

38

❧

Pennsylvania — Gravy Spackle and Stuffing Fights

Thanksgiving in Harrisburg was already heated, and the oven hadn't even preheated yet.

Why?

Because **Cousin Tyler** from Philly brought **"Philly-style stuffing"** — crusty Italian bread, hot sausage, onions, attitude.

And **Aunt Donna** from Pittsburgh brought **"Western PA stuffing"** — white bread, celery, boiled egg, and ancestral righteousness.

They both set their dishes down at the table like they were about to duel.

"One's a dish," said Aunt Donna.
"The other's a *declaration of war*."

"If your stuffing doesn't bite back, it's just wet bread," replied Tyler.

The cranberry sauce jiggled in fear.

The table lineup:

- Turkey, basted in butter and Pennsylvania pride

- Mashed potatoes with a pool of gravy deep enough to baptize someone

- Green bean casserole no one actually likes but everyone expects

- And two kinds of stuffing eyeing each other like rival mascots

Meanwhile, someone passed a bottle of **Birch beer** like it was fine wine.

Then came **the gravy incident.**

Uncle Gino, trying to "help," thickened the pot with cornstarch and silence...
and turned the gravy into **spackle.**

"I was going for body," he explained.
"It's giving drywall," whispered Cousin Jade.

You had to **slice** it.
One kid tried to butter it like a roll.

Grace was delivered by **Grandpa Vince**, who started strong but trailed off into:

"...and Lord, bless the Birds — may they cover the spread."

Go Birds was echoed like an Amen.
Aunt Donna sighed audibly.

"It's not even Eagles season. It's *gravy* season."
Dessert was:

- Shoofly pie (yes, molasses is the main character)

- Pumpkin roll

- Some experimental vegan acorn tart *brought by a college freshman who clearly wasn't raised right*

The table voted on a winner.

It wasn't the tart.
That dish got **politely ghosted** like a bad Tinder date.

In the end, the Philly stuffing won by volume.
Pittsburgh's disappeared too — but mostly out of **guilt and obligation.**

Tyler called it a win.
Donna called it *"a mercy bite."*

In Pennsylvania, Thanksgiving is gravy-thick, stuffing-stacked, and slightly sports-obsessed.
Whether you're East, West, or just stuck in the middle — bring your A-game.
And maybe a backup gravy boat.

39

Rhode Island — Espresso Crimes and Cannoli Wars

Thanksgiving in Cranston was held at Aunt Carmela's two-bedroom, where **the folding chairs outnumbered the square footage.**

By noon, the kitchen was at **maximum volume**:

- One TV on the Macy's Parade

- One Bluetooth speaker blasting Dean Martin

- And Nonna yelling "MANGIA!" at anyone standing still

The first course?
Pasta. Always pasta.
Rigatoni with red sauce, meatballs, and *a single polite salad no one touched.*

Someone asked if they could "save room for turkey."
Nonna said,

"You eat like you're going to the chair."

Then walked in **Cousin Vinny** —
With a tray of **clam cakes.**
Not dessert.
Not appetizers.
Just... **clam cakes.**
Still warm. Unapologetic.

"I figured let's mix it up," he shrugged.
"Tradition needs spice."

Silence.
The rosary beads tensed up.
Someone whispered, *"He's dead to me."*

Dinner followed the usual Rhode Island chaos:

- Of course there was turkey. It's the law.

- Lasagna? Absolutely.

- Linguine with clams? Of course.

- Stuffing? "Made with sausage, because flavor."

- Sweet potatoes? "Decorative only."

Grace was a blend of Catholic guilt, kitchen heat, and a reminder that no one was getting Nonna's house in the will if they didn't kiss her cheek *before* dessert.

Dessert was the battlefield.

Vinny asked where his clam cakes should go.
Someone pointed to the trash.
Someone else pointed to the porch.

Meanwhile, Aunt Maria revealed a **homemade cannoli cake** that made grown men cry.

Vinny tried to redeem himself by offering espresso.
It was decaf.
DEC. CAF.

The tension?
Immaculate.

In Rhode Island, Thanksgiving is Italian, intense, and **no place for innovation.**
If you want dessert, bring pastry.
If you bring clam cakes, bring car keys — you're not staying long.

40

South Carolina — Grits, Grease, and Turkey Truths

Thanksgiving in Charleston started at **7:30 a.m.**
Not with grace.
Not with coffee.
But with a full-volume debate over **grits vs. rice.**

"Rice holds sauce better," said Cousin Darius.
"Grits hold *legacy,*" replied Aunt Tameka, unwrapping her cast iron skillet like it was a weapon.

Someone suggested "both."
They were exiled to the kids' table before sunrise.

Meanwhile, **Uncle Leon** had parked the deep fryer on a trailer...
in the family boatyard.

"It's got drainage and ventilation," he said.
"That's what OSHA *would* want."

The turkey was dropped in at 9:12 a.m.
By 9:13, the entire block smelled like victory, butter, and generational seasoning.

The table lineup included:

- Smoked ham so tender it had its own zip code

- Mac and cheese with five cheeses, four opinions, and one passive-aggressive note about lactose

- Collards cooked down for three hours and 85 years

- And banana pudding that **Cousin Kendra** "reimagined" with coconut milk and oat cookies

Oat. Cookies.

Uncle Leon stared at it and whispered,

"I didn't fight in three family reunions to be served *this*."

Grace was led by Grandma, who told everyone:

"Speak your thanks *and* your truth."

This was a mistake.

Cousin Lakia used her moment to confront Aunt Vern for "liking shady posts on Facebook."

Someone spilled sweet tea.
Someone else whispered, *"Here it comes."*

Dinner continued despite the tension.

Kendra's banana pudding was politely pushed to the corner of the table.
Someone slipped a Post-it on the bowl that said *"Bless your heart."*

Meanwhile, **Uncle Leon's boatyard turkey** was crowned MVP.
It was golden, crispy, and *maybe a little greasy from the pontoon fumes,* but everyone still had seconds.

Dessert (real dessert) featured:

- Proper banana pudding

- Peach cobbler

- Pound cake that could double as a dumbbell

- And the silent understanding that Kendra would be politely asked to *"focus on table decor next year."*

In South Carolina, Thanksgiving is heat, heritage, and **absolutely not a time for coconut milk experiments.**
If you're frying in a boatyard, do it right.

And if you mess with the banana pudding... *prepare to be spiritually removed.*

41

South Dakota — Jerky, Judgment, and Windy Regret

Thanksgiving in Sioux Falls began with **a weather warning and a group prayer for the pies.**

Grandpa Clyde said it best:

"If that wind takes my cherry crumble off the sill again, I'm suing nature."

Half the family showed up in snow boots.
The other half showed up in camo.
And **Cousin Wyatt** rolled in with **a mason jar full of elk jerky** and an announcement:

"Didn't have time to thaw a turkey. But I *did* shoot lunch this week."

Aunt Darla blinked.

"We already *had* a turkey."
Wyatt winked.
"But do you have lean protein and pioneer spirit?"

The answer was no.
What they had was skepticism and cornbread.

The table featured:

- Turkey (thankfully, prepped by someone more stable)

- Mashed potatoes with so much butter they were technically flammable

- Stuffing that included **craisins, which no one agreed to but no one stopped**

- And jerky, placed in the middle like a dare

Grace was led by **Grandma Elsie**, who opened with a weather report and closed with:

"Lord, help us survive the wind, the wildlife, and whatever Wyatt just brought."

Amen.

Dinner tension peaked when **Cousin Madison**, now vegan, asked what else was meat-free.

Someone passed her the salad.
Someone else passed her an apology.
Wyatt offered jerky and said:
    "Just spiritually try it."

Madison said she'd rather eat drywall.
Uncle Bud said that's *exactly* what vegan turkey tastes like.

Dessert was:

- Rhubarb pie

- Apple crisp

- Pecan tartlets

- And a "snowball cheesecake" someone left outside to chill *and forgot*

By the time they remembered it, a raccoon had taken liberties.
Grandpa Clyde called it "a tribute to frontier living."

Wyatt's jerky was left untouched except by the dog.
Who now refuses kibble.
Grandma said, *"He's got a taste for danger now."*

In South Dakota, Thanksgiving is windy, wild, and occasionally *field-dressed.*

Bring something hearty.

Respect the raccoons.

And keep your pies indoors.

42

Tennessee — Praise Breaks and Pie Judgments

Thanksgiving in Nashville kicked off with **gospel music, deep-fried everything, and Cousin Briella's "wellness tray" no one asked for.**

Briella moved back from L.A.
She now wore wide-brim hats indoors and said things like *"My energy's not dairy-friendly."*

"I brought probiotic sweet tea with elderflower notes," she smiled.
"We already *had* sweet tea," said Aunt NeNe, not smiling.
"It's got notes too — sugar and salvation."

The table was already **blessed and overloaded:**

- Fried turkey with a hot sauce halo

- Mac & cheese with six cheeses and three prayers

- Dressing that had its own legacy

- Deviled eggs in four flavors — including "smoked," "classic," "extra classic," and *"ain't nobody touching that paprika like Big Mama did"*

Grace was a **performance.**

Uncle Ray-Ray hit a whole gospel run before even saying "Amen."
The cousins harmonized the "Thank You, Lord."
The baby added *a single scream* in B flat.

Standing ovation.

Drama hit at the beverage station.

Briella set her kombucha down next to Aunt NeNe's pitcher of sweet tea.
Then someone accidentally poured a blend of both.

The result?
A glass of confusion, betrayal, and fizzing judgment.

Uncle Duke took a sip, gagged softly, and said:

"The devil is carbonated."

Mid-meal, Briella offered to "lead a digestive breathwork moment."
Everyone pretended not to hear her.
Even the baby.

She did it anyway.
Grandma said, *"Somebody hand her a biscuit so she stops talking."*

Dessert was:

- Peach cobbler

- Chess pie

- Sweet potato pie that caused someone to whisper *"this tastes like freedom"*

- And a failed oat-crust pumpkin tart that Briella claimed was "gut-friendly"

The dog licked it once and walked away.
Twice.

In Tennessee, Thanksgiving is sacred, soulful, and **not kombucha-compatible.**
Keep your deviled eggs seasoned, your playlist blessed,
And if you remix the tea, *expect gospel warfare.*

43

Texas — Brisket, Boots, and Turkey Demotion Day

Thanksgiving in Houston kicked off with **a cloud of mesquite smoke and an argument about parking that ended with "bless your truck."**

Uncle Bo rolled up with:

- A cowboy hat

- A cooler

- And **brisket** so tender it came with a warning label

"Smoked 14 hours, prayed over twice, flipped by the Holy Spirit," he said proudly.
"We still doing turkey?" someone asked.
"Not after this," he replied, slicing into it like a spiritual act.

The food lineup looked like a rodeo of deliciousness:

- Brisket (center stage, obviously)

- Turkey (quietly to the side like it knew it was about to get replaced)

- Jalapeño cornbread

- Mac & cheese that had its own zip code

- Pinto beans that slapped like a Sunday sermon

- And **green bean casserole with tortilla chip crumble** (Texas, baby)

Then came **Cousin Haley** — a recent Austin transplant who walked in wearing cowboy boots and *vibes*.
She brought a "plant-based chili alternative."

"It's tofu-based, but with cumin intention," she said.
"It's compost," whispered Grandma.

Grace was loud, heartfelt, and filled with subtle jabs.

Uncle Bo led with:

"We thank the Lord for family, freedom, and meat cooked like He intended."

Grandma added,
"And we forgive those who brought tofu... but we don't forget."

Amen.

Drama peaked when someone spotted Haley sneaking hot sauce into the pecan pie.

"It's a sweet-heat fusion," she explained.
"It's a call for help," said Aunt Patsy.

No one touched the pie.
Even the pie judged itself.

Dessert featured:

- Real pecan pie

- Sheet cake with a Texas flag on it

- Something that may have been flan but also may have been drywall

- And Blue Bell ice cream that had to be rescued from the garage freezer after a near-meltdown

Uncle Bo was crowned **Thanksgiving MVP.**
The turkey was demoted to "next day sandwich status."
Haley was gently informed that next year, she should "*just come hungry and quiet.*"

ROBERT OKINE

She nodded.
Took her chili.
Left with her pride... and all of it.

In Texas, Thanksgiving is loud, legendary, and likely smoked.
Come with brisket, leave with praise.
And if you mess with the pie, *you better have a truck waiting.*

44

Utah — Jell-O, Joy, and the Pie Chart of Judgment

Thanksgiving in Provo kicked off with *exactly* what you'd expect:

- Matching cardigans

- A spreadsheet of seating assignments

- And **Sister-in-Law Claire** bringing four varieties of Jell-O salad, all green, all glowing, and all named after virtues

"This one's 'Gratitude,'" she smiled.
"That one's 'Fellowship.'"
"The one with marshmallows is 'Endurance.'"

Uncle Russell whispered, *"That one's 'intestinal warfare.'"*

The buffet was organized like a youth retreat:

- Turkey (carved with reverence and nitrile gloves)

- Funeral potatoes (ironically cheerful)

- Homemade rolls that had risen more than Cousin Trevor's testimony

- A veggie tray shaped like the Temple

- And Jell-O.
  So much Jell-O.

One had shredded carrots.
One had cottage cheese.
One was just... *blue.*

Grace was **a full family devotion**, led by Grandma Ruth and accompanied by **Cousin Mallory on ukulele.**

Midway through, someone tried to harmonize.
Someone else tried to clap.
Grandpa Eldon just whispered,

"We used to eat in silence and fear. I miss that."
Drama peaked during Pie Placement.
Cousin Ethan (age 9) was self-appointed Pie Organizer.
He arranged them into categories:

- "Traditional & Blessed" (pumpkin, pecan, apple)

- "Experimental but Repentable" (sugar-free options)

- "Unholy Offerings" (gluten-free bean-based abomination from the neighbor's missionary girlfriend)

Ethan placed a Post-it on the bean pie that said:

"I rebuke thee."

Later, someone tried to start a **Thanksgiving hymn singalong.**
Only two people knew the words.
Three pretended.
Uncle Russell turned on the football game from his phone under the table.

He was not rebuked.
He was thanked.

Dessert was orderly.
Until Claire tried to stack the Jell-O salads.
They collapsed into a shimmering avalanche of lime, orange, and regret.

Grandma Ruth said,

"The Lord gives and the Lord gelatineth."

In Utah, Thanksgiving is sweet, sacred, and slightly sticky.
Come with good intentions, clear containers,
and if you bring Jell-O, *just know someone's watching.*

45

Vermont — Maple, Haikus, and the Pie Purse Miracle

Thanksgiving in Montpelier began with **fog, flannel, and a handwritten menu nailed to a reclaimed barn plank.**

Host?
Cousin Wren.
Moved off-grid in April.
Now runs a mindfulness retreat for alpacas.

"This year," Wren whispered, "we're hosting a *Low-Impact, High-Vibration Gratitude Ceremony.*"

Uncle Everett whispered back,

"So... no gravy?"

The menu was artisanal chaos:

- Heritage turkey from a farm called *"Whispering Thistle"*

- Roasted root vegetables "in their own story arc"

- Maple-glazed quinoa loaf

- Stuffing made with sourdough and *light judgment*

- And kombucha served in old jam jars labeled "thankful-ness fizz"

Then **Aunt Beth** arrived — with a **plastic tub of Stove Top** and a bottle of Vermont maple syrup from a warehouse with fluorescent lighting and zero shame.

Wren gasped.

"This isn't small-batch!"
Beth replied,
"Neither am I, honey."

Grace began with a **gong**.
Then Wren stood and recited:

Gratitude flows in
Whispers of cranberry light
Pass the root, not rage.

A haiku.
Instead of prayer.
Instead of pie.

Uncle Everett coughed and said,

"Can someone pass the rage anyway?"

The turkey was juicy.
The kombucha was divisive.
And the sweet potatoes came with a backstory longer than a novel.

Then came dessert.

There was:

- Maple-nut tartlets

- Apple crisp made with apples "rescued from capitalist neglect"

- One mysterious vegan "butterless butter square"

- And no pie.

NO. PIE.

Grandma Fern, who'd been quiet all evening, stood up.
Pulled out a pie from her purse.
A full, still-warm pumpkin pie wrapped in a crocheted doily.

Everyone cheered.
Someone played wind chimes.

Wren sighed and said,

"I guess the universe wanted balance."

In Vermont, Thanksgiving is poetic, plant-based, and occasionally passive-aggressive.
Bring your own pie.
Respect the root vegetables.
And if someone starts haiku-ing, *just say "mmm" and pass the butter.*

46

◦❦◦

Virginia — Biscuits, Bravado, and Founding Fathers

T hanksgiving in Williamsburg started with **a reenactment.**

Cousin Clark, who did a semester in Boston and now insists he's *"Southern by heritage"*, greeted guests in full colonial garb.

"Welcome, kinfolk. On this day of harvest—"
"Clark," Grandma said, "stop talking like Hamilton and grab the mashed potatoes."

The spread was presidential:

- Buttered rolls with names like *"Jefferson's Crust"*

- Green beans *not touched by almonds or anyone under 30*

- Turkey (brined and basted in *ancestral pride*)

- Sweet potatoes so rich they came with a trust fund

- And mac & cheese baked like a constitutional right

Drama started early when **Clark tried to lead a "Founding Fathers Thanksgiving Toast."**

He raised a glass and said,

"To liberty, land, and low-gluten stuffing!"

Aunt Renee replied,

"To Clark going back to Connecticut."

Then **Cousin Ava** walked in wearing an apron that said "Bless This Southern Mess" — she's from New Jersey.
No one said anything.
But someone **rearranged her place card to the folding chair at the end.**

Grace was a moment of peace... until Clark started quoting Thomas Jefferson mid-prayer.

Grandpa said,

"The only founding father I care about today is whoever invented sweet tea."

Aunt Renee clapped.
Someone passed a casserole like it was an agreement.

Dessert included:

- Apple pie (with a flag-shaped crust)

- Pecan pie (with bourbon and vengeance)

- Cornbread pudding

- And one ambitious fig tart Clark made using a *"colonial recipe scroll"* printed from Pinterest

No one ate the tart.
Even the dog refused.

Clark tried to give a speech about "what Thanksgiving means to true Americans."

Grandma said,

"What it means is you do dishes if you didn't cook."

Clark disappeared shortly after that.
His hat was found on a biscuit tray.

In Virginia, Thanksgiving is historical, heartfelt, and **not your moment to audition for Broadway.**

Mind your manners.
Mind your accent.
And don't test Grandma if you want seconds.

47

Washington — Espresso Birds and Costco Redemption

Thanksgiving in Seattle started with fog, flannel, and **Cousin Skyler** saying:

"This year, we're focusing on *elevated flavor profiles.*"

Translation:
The turkey was **espresso-rubbed**, *not* "dry," just "aromatic."
The stuffing had dried cranberries and *intent.*
The green beans were cold "on purpose."
And the pie crust was gluten-free, dairy-free, and **joy-free.**

The vibe at the table?

- Cozy, polite, *and emotionally withheld.*

- Aunt Nora brought her own wine opener and a tote bag labeled "Self-Care."

- Uncle Max brought his opinions and an IPA he brewed himself, named "Gravy Angst."

Grace was short, whispered, and mostly drowned out by **a curated lo-fi playlist.**
Then Skyler stood and said,

"Before we eat, I'd love to share the turkey's journey."

Grandma blinked.

"If it didn't cross a river with Moses, I don't care."

Drama hit when Grandpa Al asked for gravy.

Skyler replied,

"There's a mushroom jus with a miso finish."

Al stared.
Took a sip.

"Tastes like compost water."

Meanwhile, **Cousin Molly** kept referring to her stuffing as "plant-forward,"
but everyone else called it *"wheat paste with raisins."*

The wine, however, was flowing.
And so were the feelings.

By the time dessert hit, **someone had already cried in the mud-room.**
(Just once. Respectfully.)

Dessert included:

- A vegan pumpkin tart

- A rustic pear galette "built with mindfulness"

- And a full **Costco pumpkin pie** that Aunt Nora brought "just in case Seattle got too experimental"

Grandma went straight for the Costco pie.
Said,

"Now that's America."

Skyler tried to start a gratitude circle.
Uncle Max said,

"I'm grateful y'all aren't in charge of dinner next year."
Mic. Dropped.

In Washington, Thanksgiving is refined, rain-washed, and *weirdly caffeinated.*

Bring a beanie, bring your boundaries,
And don't put espresso on the bird unless you're *ready for critique and therapy.*

48

⚮

West Virginia — Moonshine and the Mashed Mic Drop

Thanksgiving in Charleston was held at Aunt Jolene's — who lives **halfway up a mountain**, owns **five crockpots**, and once declared *"deviled eggs are a spiritual experience."*

This year's theme?
"Traditional with flair."
The flair?
Moonshine.
In. Everything.

The food lineup:

- Deep-fried turkey with hot honey glaze

- Mashed potatoes whipped so smooth they *started rumors*

- Cornbread so crumbly it needed a warning label

- Mac & cheese "thick enough to patch a coal tunnel"

- And collard greens with a dash of — you guessed it — moonshine

Cousin Tanner arrived late...
Wearing a leather jacket and carrying a gravy boat filled with something clear, strong, and **questionably legal.**

"It's a 'gratitude tonic,'" he said.
"It's a DUI," muttered Aunt Jolene.

Grace was led by **Papaw Buck**, who gave thanks for:

- Family

- Clean socks

- And "the strength to not slap anyone this year"

Amen came with a banjo strum.

Then came the chaos.

Tanner started pouring **moonshine "gravy"** over everything.
Even the pumpkin pie.
Even the deviled eggs.

Grandma gasped.
Someone dropped a ham.
Papaw Buck took a sip and said,

"Tastes like regret and lightning. I love it."

The fight broke out over **who made the best mashed potatoes.**

Aunt Jolene: "I use heavy cream and emotional consistency."
Cousin Sherry: "Mine have rosemary and peace."
Tanner: "I added whiskey to mine."
Uncle Merle: "You added jail time."

Dessert included:

- Bourbon pecan pie

- Apple crisp with extra crisp and extra bourbon

- Pumpkin pie that had *nothing infused in it and won Dessert MVP by unanimous vote*

- And a single "keto mountain muffin" that nobody acknowledged

After dinner, someone pulled out a fiddle.
Someone else pulled a hamstring trying to two-step.
The moonshine ran out around midnight.

Tanner was last seen blessing the gravy boat and promising to start a YouTube channel.

In West Virginia, Thanksgiving is loud, lit, and a little lawless.
Bring real gravy.
Respect the deviled eggs.
And if you spike the pie, *be ready to square dance with Jesus.*

49

Wisconsin — Beer Sauce, Brats, and Grandma's Nod

Thanksgiving in Madison started with **snow, snark, and stretchy pants.**
Uncle Jerry rolled in holding a crockpot and said:

"If there's no cheese in your stuffing, I don't trust your politics."

Everyone nodded.
Everyone understood.

The table was dairy-forward and emotionally rich:

- Turkey (smoked with hickory and hope)

- Mashed potatoes with *three sticks of butter, minimum*

- Stuffing that squeaked when you chewed (thanks, cheese curds)

- Green beans with *ranch dust and defiance*

- And **"cran-beer sauce"** — made with lager, spite, and *someone's home brew*

Then came **Cousin Derek**, late as usual —
carrying a foil-wrapped tray like it held state secrets.

"I brought bratwursts. Beer-braised. Grilled on the porch. You're welcome."

A hush fell over the room.
Then a cheer.
A child may have wept.

Grace was delivered by **Grandma Bev**, who opened with:

"Lord, thank you for cheese, strong hearts, and stronger livers."

Uncle Jerry added,

"And the Packers, even when they test us."

The drama?
The *vegan cauliflower gratin* brought by someone's new girlfriend.

It was... fine.
But next to the five-cheese mac?
Invisible.

Someone put a Post-it on it that said *"participation appreciated."*

Dessert featured:

- Cheesecake

- Pumpkin pie with whipped cream shaped like Lambeau Field

- Cranberry bars "for texture"

- And **a vat of homemade custard** that came with no instructions and full consequences

Derek's bratwursts?
Gone in 10 minutes.
He got a plate made just for him.
Grandma Bev whispered,

"He's not perfect, but he's got taste."

In Wisconsin, Thanksgiving is cheesy, chilly, and **curd-powered.**
If it squeaks, it's sacred.
And if you bring bratwurst, you bring peace.

50

Wyoming — Blizzards, Bison, and a Side of Shade

Thanksgiving in Casper started with **four trucks stuck in a snowdrift** and a group text that read:

"Do we plow or do we pray?"

Grandpa said, *"The Lord helps those with snow tires."*

Inside, the wood stove was roaring, the Wi-Fi was "iffy," and **Uncle Wade was already mad** that someone brought tofu.

"That thing doesn't moo or matter," he muttered, stirring chili with a power drill.

Yes. **A power drill.**

The menu? Frontier fabulous:

- Turkey? Yes.

- Bison roast? Also yes.

- Elk sausage? Probably legal.

- Mashed potatoes with ranch seasoning and attitude

- Green bean casserole with crushed Doritos because *tradition evolves*

Then **Cousin Jess** — fresh back from "one semester of environmental science" — declared:

"We shouldn't be eating bison. They're spiritual creatures."

Uncle Wade replied,

"This one's *delicious*. Bless its spirit twice."

Grace was delivered by **Grandma Wanda**, who wore camo and Crocs and still somehow commanded respect.

"Lord, thank you for meat, warmth, and not living anywhere with traffic."

Everyone clapped.
Even the casserole jiggled with approval.

The drama?
The generator died mid-dessert.

Power went out.
So did patience.
Grandpa lit three lanterns.
Uncle Wade said it "felt authentic."

Jess tried to do a spoken-word poem about food justice.
Someone passed her a roll and said, *"Read the room, sweetie."*

Dessert was rustic and righteous:

- Huckleberry pie

- Dutch oven cobbler

- S'mores made on the wood stove

- One rogue chia pudding someone slipped in from "the city" (and immediately exiled)

In Wyoming, Thanksgiving is snowy, smoky, and **exactly as wild as it should be.**
Bring boots, bring butter,
And don't argue with the guy cooking meat in Carhartt and prayer.

51

D.C. — Drumsticks, Diplomacy, & a Side of Scandal

Thanksgiving in the nation's capital kicked off with **an itinerary.**
Sent in advance.
With bullet points.
And a color-coded seating chart that **accidentally grouped Republicans near the vegan chili.**

"Let's focus on unity," said Aunt Cynthia, distributing bipartisan pie forks.

The guest list included:

- Two lawyers

- One lobbyist

- A campaign intern with a 37-slide Google Deck about gratitude

- And Grandma Rose, who told everyone she was "independent, but not afraid to throw a sandal if provoked."

The food?
Heavily debated.

Turkey: ethically sourced
Stuffing: gluten-flexible
Mac & cheese: under Congressional review
Cranberry sauce:

"We'll be voting on that," said Uncle Paul.
"Canned or fresh?"
"Both sides must be heard."

Grace started strong...
...until Cousin Zion added a land acknowledgment, a climate action plan, and **two policy suggestions**.

Uncle Greg stood up and yelled,

"I just wanted mashed potatoes and silence!"

He did not get either.

Then came the Drumstick Dispute.

There were two.
Three claimants.
And one toddler holding a plastic gavel yelling *"ORDER!"*

The group proposed a rotational model.
Grandma Rose said,

"I'm taking both. I raised you all."

Case closed.

Dessert was:

- Pumpkin pie (fact-checked)

- Apple pie (in a commemorative pie dish from the Obama years)

- A fruit salad someone brought from Capitol Hill labeled *"Bipartisan Compromise"*

No one touched it.

Tension finally broke when someone played the Electric Slide.

All sides danced.
No debates.
Just joyful chaos and a spilled pitcher of sparkling cider.

Grandma Rose led.
In heels.
With a napkin tucked in her neckline like a true patriot.

In D.C., Thanksgiving is political, polished, and perfectly over-scheduled.
Come hungry, stay neutral,
And don't fight Grandma for the last drumstick — **she's already three steps ahead.**

52

The Things We Don't Say at the Table (But Should)

We gather every year like it's a tradition (because it is). We pass the gravy.
We pass the rolls.
We pass **judgment**, ever so gently, tucked inside a "How's work?" or "You still seeing that boy?"

But what we don't pass?

The real stuff.

Here's what we *meant* to say but didn't — across all 50 states and one very spicy D.C.:

"Yes, the mac and cheese is different. You did your best. We love you anyway."

But instead we said:

"Oh... interesting texture."

"I forgive you for what you said in 2009 about my deviled eggs. But I do remember."

Instead we said:

"Need any help in the kitchen?"
(Translation: I'm watching you.)

"That casserole you bring every year? No one eats it. We just shift it around the buffet line like a hot potato of politeness."

But out loud?

"You brought it again! Wow!"

"Grandma, we know who really makes the turkey. You just supervise now. And that's okay. You're still MVP."

But we said:

"This bird tastes just like last year's!"
(Which was also supervised.)

"I'm not actually mad at you — I just didn't know how to say I missed you."

Instead:

"So... how's work?"
And a half hug that said *"please don't let go too fast."*

**"I'm tired. I'm hurting. I'm healing. I wish we could be real
without ruining the stuffing."**

But we said:

"Can you pass the rolls?"
And hoped someone heard the *crack* in our voice under the butter
knife.

**"I'm proud of you. No matter what. You survived. And showed
up."**

Instead?

"You want leftovers?"

Which is love.
In a Tupperware container.
With your name Sharpie'd on top.

In every state, at every table, there are things we don't say —
Because we're scared they'll break the silence.
But maybe, just maybe... they'll fix everything else.

So next year?
Say the thing.
And then pass the pie.

53

The Turkey Is Not the Only Thing Getting Roasted

So here we are.
Fifty states. One District.
A hundred kinds of stuffing, a thousand things unsaid, and **one very emotional cranberry sauce**.

We've laughed.
We've judged.
We've passed dishes we didn't like to people we love — and that's the most Thanksgiving thing of all.

Because here's the truth:
Thanksgiving isn't about perfection.
It's not about crisp turkey skin, the correct pie ratio, or whether Cousin Sharon brought her weird "detox yams" *again*.

It's about **showing up**.

Hungry.

Grateful-ish.

Ready to love people who drive you nuts.

And if this book has reminded you of someone —
A family member.
A friend.
A dinner that went sideways but *still somehow stuck in your heart...*

Then I've done my job.

And maybe next Thanksgiving...
you'll roast a little less.
Laugh a little more.
And remember that no matter how weird, wild, or well-seasoned
your family is...

You're not the only one.
Now close the book, grab a fork, and go tell someone,
"I saved you the last piece."

About the Author

Robert Okine is the kind of guy who reads state laws for fun and critiques pie crusts like a Food Network judge. A global nomad with a knack for finding the absurd in the ordinary, he's turned his observations of American life into bestselling social satires that are as insightful as they are hilarious.

When he's not roasting Thanksgiving traditions, he's dissecting grocery store aisle quirks and canine privileges across the fifty states in his *USA The Land With At Least 50 Options™* series.

He lives in Washington, D.C., drinks his coffee black, and believes every family dinner should come with a side of laughter—and maybe a fire extinguisher.

Other Books by Robert Okine

Available in paperback, hardcover, eBook, and audiobook formats wherever books are sold.

USA: The Land With At Least 50 Options
A hilarious, eye-opening tour of America—one grocery aisle at a time. Discover the quirks, cravings, and culture of all 50 states through sharp wit and curiosity.

Available in paperback, hardcover, eBook, and audiobook formats wherever books are sold.

USA: Where Dogs Have More Rights Than You Do
A hilarious and eye-opening tour of America's states — one barking mad, bone-laced, paw-approved policy at a time.

Coming Soon from Robert Okine

- **50 Ways to Say "I Do" and Still Argue About the Dishes**
  Love, marriage, and epic debates—explored state by state.

- **One Nation, 50 Ways to Live Your Best Life**
  An uplifting, big-hearted guide to chasing happiness across America.

Stay in the loop:
For upcoming books, bonus content, and exclusive updates, visit:
www.therobertokine.com

Thank you for reading, sharing, and supporting indie authors!

Did This Book Make You Snort-Laugh Over Stuffing?

Leave a Review—It's the Gravy on Top!

If you enjoyed *The Turkey Isn't the Only Thing Getting Roasted*, I'd be truly thankful if you left a quick review.

Whether it was your favorite dysfunctional dinner, an unhinged casserole moment, or how many times you said "this is *my* family"... every review helps other readers find the book and join the feast.

You can leave a review **wherever you purchased your copy—**Amazon, Goodreads, Apple Books, Kobo, Barnes & Noble, or any platform that tickled your funny bone.

Reviews support indie authors, spread laughter, and keep the holiday chaos alive—one chapter, one chuckle, one five-star pie at a time.

Thanks for pulling up a chair.

With gratitude,

Robert Okine

www.ingramcontent.com/pod-product-compliance
Lightning Source LLC
Chambersburg PA
CBHW060418130626
46555CB00005B/2122

* 9 7 9 8 9 9 9 8 6 5 1 2 4 3 *